UNPLUG
YOUR
Kids

A Parent's Guide to Raising Happy, Active, and Well-Adjusted Children in the Digital Age

David Dutwin, Ph.D.

Adamsmedia
Avon, Massachusetts

Copyright © 2009 by David Dutwin, Ph.D.
All rights reserved.
This book, or parts thereof, may not be reproduced in any
form without permission from the publisher; exceptions are
made for brief excerpts used in published reviews.

Published by
Adams Media, an F+W Media Company
57 Littlefield Street, Avon, MA 02322. U.S.A.
www.adamsmedia.com

ISBN 10: 1-59869-804-4
ISBN 13: 978-1-59869-804-6

Printed in the United States of America.

J I H G F E D C B A

Library of Congress Cataloging-in-Publication Data
is available from the publisher.

This publication is designed to provide accurate and authoritative information
with regard to the subject matter covered. It is sold with the understanding that
the publisher is not engaged in rendering legal, accounting, or other professional
advice. If legal advice or other expert assistance is required, the services of a
competent professional person should be sought.
—From a *Declaration of Principles* jointly adopted by a Committee of the
American Bar Association and a Committee of Publishers and Associations

Many of the designations used by manufacturers and sellers to distinguish their
product are claimed as trademarks. Where those designations appear in this book
and Adams Media was aware of a trademark claim, the designations have been
printed with initial capital letters.

This book is available at quantity discounts for bulk purchases.
For information, please call 1-800-289-0963.

Contents

Acknowledgments

WRITING A BOOK means that other things must be pushed aside, which subsequently means, when one is raising two very young boys, that someone has to take up the slack. As if she wasn't already! But suffice to say, thanks to my wife Betsy for taking up the slack! Some of you may appreciate the fact that, well, two boys are a handful! Thanks to my mom as well for the background work and grammatical review.

A book like this is a rarity. It is so much easier for publishers to play it safe and publish the books that have the flashy titles and the extreme points of view. Such books are so much easier to market and sell. It is much more difficult to publish a book that eschews the lure of fast money with quick headlines, and instead tells the ugly truth: Life is complicated. And the effects of the media on your children is no less complicated of an issue than most other issues you face throughout life. But there is clarity in knowledge. That is what this book is about: Infusing you with knowledge on the bad and the good of the media and children, regardless of whether it produces flashy headlines. This book tells readers the simple facts in a straightforward way and offers advice that works for working folks. It's a much tougher sell, and I am thankful Adams Media saw fit to take on the challenge and report the truth.

Introduction

AS A PROFESSIONAL research scholar, I have come to realize that I am a glutton for punishment, or at least, that is what my friends and family think. What I am speaking about is my "pleasure reading" of academic journal articles about research on children and media, as well as other topics. If you have never read or even seen an academic journal article, you probably want to keep it that way. They are dense, riddled with statistics, and probably even more often, written with the intent to confuse the reader; what academics call "academic gobedellygook." No, these are not the Michael Crichton's of the world writing these articles. Bluntly put, there are a lot of incredibly talented researchers out there with less than desirable writing skills!

As a research scholar, I suppose I have become somewhat impervious to the bad writing. To me, discovering what people have learned, and learning about how they figured things out, is fun and exciting. So when I first got interested in the effects of the mass media on children, as a professional researcher, I went straight to the source: The academic journal articles and books written by people who actually did the research necessary to figure out what the media is doing to our kids.

What I found in the vast volume of research conducted on the effects of media on children is this: Kids of all ages consume quite a bit of media, and, mostly, they turn out just fine. There are certain aspects of the media that can teach kids all sorts of knowledge and skills and promote personal growth. And, there are certain aspects of the media that can hurt your children in a myriad of ways, from suppressing learning to stunting personal growth.

Let me be even clearer about that: The vast majority of children who watch a lot of television, play a lot of video games, and spend a lot of time with a computer turn out just fine. However, kids are not dice. You can go to Las Vegas and bet all you want on small odds to "win it all," and there is nothing wrong with that. But if you are like most parents, you are always looking for ways to protect your kids. Do you really want to take risks with your children's health and well-being? No, none of us do.

So how do you protect them? This book is written to provide you the answers. A message that runs throughout the book is that the first step in protecting your kids from any threat begins with knowledge about that threat. But furthermore, because a substantial amount of research finds positive effects of media on kids, you don't want to throw out the proverbial baby with the bathwater. Better to use some forms of media to advance your kids developmentally, while limiting other forms of media when needed to prevent possible stunting of their development. This book tells you when to worry, when to relax, how to protect, and how to promote. We all agree that the media can have a tremendous impact on children. Why not learn to maximize its positive effects and minimize the bad?

Given that if you are interested enough in this topic (and I think this topic is important enough that *all* parents should be interested), and you are reading this introduction, there is a chance you might have come across some other books that purportedly talk about this same topic. If so, I would like to give you fair warning that there are two types of people that tend to write these kinds of books, as I alluded to in my acknowledgments. The first is a researcher who sets out to find the truth. The second is the author who has it in their head that media is either the most wonderful thing that has ever happened to humankind, or is the worse thing to ever happen to young children. This second type of person is not interested in finding the truth, but rather is solely interested in forcing facts and statistics to conform to their way of thinking.

You, I hope, are reading this not because you already know it all. You don't want to be lectured; you want to be spoken to. You are reading this because you want the truth.

So, welcome to my book. I think you will find a lot of interesting and useful information here. Our goal is to figure out what we really should do as parents in our media-saturated world, to understand this media as well as our children do, to protect them by informing ourselves about the things that could hurt them. We teach our children to ride a bike and drive a car in a safe way, correct? As so many exemplars have shown us, from Columbine and beyond, we need to treat media the same way we treat a car: with respect. We must also have an understanding that we cannot really control what our kids do with such instruments but we can instill in them the values to make rational and smart decisions when using such things.

So let's get started.

Media and Kids

A FEW MONTHS AGO, my wife called me to ask that I stop by the local toy store to get a "Vtech" cartridge. In a hurry at the time, I did not stop to ask exactly what this meant, but I figured someone at the store would help me out. Once at the store I was shown to the wall of Vtech cartridges available and selected two from the racks. From the logo, I surmised that these were cartridges to an interactive book we had.

Little did I realize, I was buying my son's first video game!

It turns out the Vtech system is a video game system not unlike its older siblings, Playstation, Nintendo, and Xbox 360. Only cuter, of course (orange and chubby, but still, your basic video game console).

The funny thing was that one of the last kernels of information I was looking for when preparing this book was an answer to this question: When do most families destined to own a video game system purchase their first console? Well, it looks like I found out when! I had thought the child would be perhaps six to eight years old. Turns out we bought it when he was exactly four years, three months.

It was quite a rewarding experience, as it turns out. The speed at which my son "caught on" to the goals of the games was exciting. In fact, thus far in his life there have been few other instances of such "instant learning gratification" where I was able to witness such an immediate learning curve with palpable and measurable results.

This got me thinking about video games. After all, about ninety percent, if not ninety-eight percent, of all research on video games appears to be patently negative. In a sense, what I witnessed was the potential power of learning that can occur from video games: They are interactive, colorful, and filled with activities that present immediate feedback that include color, sound, and all sorts of game-imbedded rewards such as points. What's not to like here? In a sense, video games seemed the perfect learning medium, one where all the complexities of life can be whittled down to the most simple of tasks: Get the letter "B" from the little birdie on the screen and you will be rewarded!

Then again, is it realistic to whittle away so much of life's complexities? Am I just getting my child hooked on yet another video screen activity? Isn't four years old much too young, despite what I witnessed? (Which was a kid ripe for learning and interacting in exactly the way video games seemed to offer.)

And finally, the most burning question of all: Is this *Thomas and Friends Letter Train* just the first step to some future play, acting out of some ultraviolent action game (say, the hypothetical *Grand Theft Auto 12: How to Kill Cops Best and Get Away with It*)?

Unfortunately, there are plenty of people out there saying "yes" to such questions. Indeed, I have already lost credibility with any reader out there suspicious of such arguments. The answer isn't found in our feelings and suspicions about what media can do to our kids. The answer to such questions is found in good, solid research on the topic.

The Importance of Research

It is important to pause and talk about why this is true. Research, mostly founded in the scientific method, is a process of exploring the world to uncover truth about it. Long ago, philosophers and the first budding scientists of the enlightenment realized that quite a bit of what humans thought was "true" about the world was not really true (you know, like that the earth was the center of the solar system). They began to realize that to really find the truth, they needed to first understand why we find falsehoods. The answer is that there are a lot of things about you and me that are quite imperfect. We tend to let first impressions unduly rule our judgment. We stereotype. We let our feelings, our egos, get in the way of sound decision making. We accept what others tell us on faith alone.

What was needed, then, was a method to eliminate the impact of these imperfections we all have. Today this is known as the scientific method.

This method is by no means perfect. But it is the most accurate and reliable method we have to discover truth about the world. This method employs surveys, interviews, and experiments to explore the effects that one thing has on another—for example, the effect media have on children. Or more specifically, the effect violent television programming has on the number of aggressive thoughts your teen has throughout the day. And that is just one example. Today, research scholars have asked hundreds of similar questions pertaining to the effects of the mass media on our kids.

As I will mention time and again, the scientific method always aims to answer two questions: First, is there a scientifically detectable effect of one thing (educational television, for example) on another (preschooler learning)? Second, if there is an effect, how much of an effect is there? In other words, will my kids learn just a few words from a pro-vocabulary learning television show, or hundreds?

The Method of Research

How do scientists figure out how the media can affect us? There are typically three ways scientists research media effects. First of all, researchers look at what is actually *in* the media. It is easy enough for pundits to chalk up all media as ultraviolent and awash with sexual content, but scientists don't operate that way. They need to know for sure. Thus, what they do is gather a lot of media, for example, every magazine from the top ten magazines for the last ten years, and page by page, actually measure to what degree they contain violent or sexual content compared to nonviolent or nonsexual content.

Once researchers know what media actually consist of, they can begin to study their potential effects. One way to do this is to survey people. In short, they will ask people questions about their media consumption patterns as well as their likelihood to be aggressive, or hold sexual stereotypes, or, in the case of young children, whether they have attention problems or sleep problems. If the right kind of media use is high (for example, a person watches not just a lot of media but specifically a lot of violent content) in some people and not others, and those same people are also found to have more aggressive tendencies than other people, then researchers say there is a correlation between violent television watching and having aggressive attitudes. However, the problem with correlations is they do not prove that one thing causes another. Indeed, it very well may be the case that people with aggressive tendencies seek out violent television, not that violent television makes people aggressive. Luckily, researchers can use mathematical models to statistically rule out other factors. For example, having aggressive parents might actually be the key factor leading to aggressive children, and when this factor is put into the analysis, the supposed effect of violent television could disappear. Still, it is sometimes difficult for researchers to measure every possible other explanation, and thus correlational research always has to be judged based on the thoroughness with which researchers think things through and control for other possible explanations.

Finally, researchers conduct experiments. Experiments have the advantage of being able to show causality. For example, researchers can take a group of people and randomly put them into two groups. The first group watches nonviolent television, and the second group watches violent television. The advantage here is because people were randomly assigned to one or the other group, any pre-existing tendency toward aggression is evenly distributed into both groups, and thus cannot be a factor in the research. After each group watches a specific type of programming (violent or nonviolent), the experimenters can ask them to do a task, or fill out a questionnaire. For example, they could ask the respondents, on a scale of one to ten, how much they think yelling is appropriate to sometimes solve your problems. If the people who watched the violent programming in the experiment give higher scores than those who watched nonviolent television, then the experiment has shown that television is not just associated or correlated with aggressive tendencies but also can actually cause aggressive tendencies as well. If there is one major problem with experiments, it is that they often are measuring behavior in an experimental or artificial setting. Would people react the same way if they watched violent television at home? Secondly, experimenters usually measure whether the two groups act different or answer questions differently at some point right after the end of their watching of violent or nonviolent media. Meaning, they are left unsure if whether the watching of violent television would have any lasting impact.

Despite these shortcomings, research on media effects has been very successful. Because media has been with us for so many decades, researchers have had a chance to study most major potential effects in many different ways. In other words, if one survey or one experiment found a link between violent television and aggressive thoughts, one could find enough flaws in that single study to potentially discredit it. The lack of other studies to back that information up could reduce confidence that what it found is actually true. But when the same topic is studied in five different surveys and five different experiments, and nine out of ten of these research projects all find a link between violent television and aggressive thoughts, then one can be quite confident that the researchers are on to something. And for many of the topics studied by media scholars, there have indeed been numerous studies on the same topics over the years.

Reporting on Research

If there is one serious problem with research, it is that journalists don't seem to be able to effectively report on research in a way that gives ordinary people the facts they need. Typically, when research comes out showing a bad effect of the mass media, it gets pretty good news coverage. Why the press? Because it sells papers.

The problem is that reporters, as I have touched on earlier, don't understand enough about research to understand what the research really means. Researchers attempt to find differences that are "statistically significant." This means that mathematically, they find that one thing (violent media content) is associated with another (aggressive thoughts). But most reporters and researchers alike fail to ask the next question, which is: What does the finding mean in the real world? A lot of research, while "statistically significant," translates into a minor, at best, impact in the real world. As I will discuss in the next chapter, for example, researchers Christakis and Zimmerman have indeed found a mathematical link between watching TV under the age of two and developing attentional problems by age seven. But when one looks at what the math means in the real world, we find out that ten percent of seven-year-olds have attention problems. For every hour of television watched above the average amount of television watched for a two year old, a child becomes one percent more likely to develop problems paying attention. So now, it's eleven percent. A difference? Yes. Worthy of major headlines? Probably not. Part of the goal of this book is to not just report the facts, but to do so in a way that anyone can understand, and to do so in a way that translates the statistics into everyday, "on the ground" realities.

The Problem with Averages

Another reason research sometimes gets more "weight" than it should is because news outlets love reporting averages. How many hours of television, for example, do our children watch? What we are given is the national average. It is important to note, however, that the "average" amount of television is a tricky little statistic. Think of children playing at the seesaw. Imagine for a second there is one child who is sure to become the next hall of fame lineman for the Green Bay Packers. Big kid. Now on the other side is your average or even a bit undersized child. What happens on the seesaw? Absolutely nothing, right? The big kid is just too big. The little kid jumps up and down on his side and nothing happens. The seesaw is standing straight up in the air. So what does he do? He gets his friends, of course. And after three more of his friends pile on to their side of the seesaw, finally, it begins to budge. Add one more, and the seesaw balances, and starts to go up and down, up and down.

That is exactly what happens when one calculates averages and there are "extra heavy" numbers on the high end of the scale. In order to find that perfect midpoint, many more people have to be on one end to balance the few big kids on the other. And such is the case with the average number of television hours watched. It turns out there are a few kids out there on the extreme end of television viewing, while (they watch ten or more hour per day) many, many more children watching less than an hour per day on the other end.

Type of Truth Research Finds

Finally, it will perhaps help you make sense out of the research I report in the book if I describe the types of findings researchers usually look for. There are three main types of findings that I will allude to now and again in this book. The first is "knowledge," and I put the term in quotes for a very specific reason, because what I am referring to is what people *think* they know. For example, how many violent crimes happen in your town? How many 16-year-olds have had sexual intercourse? These are probably more accurately referred to as opinions people have, but then again, they are sometimes so sure of what they think they know that I refer to it as personal knowledge. So the question is, do media affect what we think we know? For example, do kids who watch a lot of sexual content think that more 16-year-olds have had sex than kids who watch very little sexual content?

Second, researchers look at attitudes. Continuing with the same example, do kids who watch a lot of sexual content end up holding more permissive attitudes about sex than kids who don't watch a lot of sexual content? And finally, there is behavior. Does watching sexual content actually lead to an earlier initiation of sexual behavior? These three effects, knowledge and opinion, attitudes, and behavior, constitute increasing degrees of effect. In other words, it is one thing for media to convince us the world is violent. It is yet another to make someone have aggressive attitudes toward others. And it is another matter entirely if media can persuade people to act violently. Collectively, the body of research out there looks at each of these levels on each area of concern.

Areas of Concern

You will find that each chapter has sections particular to certain types of media. The media reviewed in this book are:

Television: To ease writing and facilitate the readability of this book, television throughout is the term I will use—not only television programming but DVDs and movie watching on a television. True, a DVD children's program can be watched on either a television, DVD player/viewer (such as in the car), or a computer. All of this is generally included under the guise of television research. In later chapters, movies will be broken out as a separate category since the research begins to focus on movies differently than television as kids grow older.

Music: From any nonscreen watching source such as a car radio, MP3 player, or even live performance.

Computers and the Internet: Generally, this includes any screen time dedicated to the computer, with the exception of television programs on DVDs and movies on DVDs.

Video Games: These can be played on either computer or television monitors.

Advertising: As you might guess, this includes ALL advertising regardless of the medium.

The Game Plan

This book unfolds in a rather straightforward fashion. Each chapter addresses a specific life stage children go through, ranging from babies and toddlers to high schoolers. Within each chapter, relevant topics are discussed. Each chapter starts with traditional screen media (television, DVDs, and movies), and then moves to computers and the Internet, video games, advertising, and finally, music. Not all chapters have these sections, however, since for some age groups there is not really anything to discuss on the topic. Topics tend to be cumulative, meaning that just because violent video games are discussed in the chapter on preteens, this does not mean that the danger goes away for middle school students. Indeed, it is probably more likely that your middle school child plays violent video games than does your early tween. But the book is structured to teach parents to foster discussion before such behavior or problems become prevalent, rather than to wait until after they have set in.

This book is designed to be more than just a factual guide with tips to overcome the potential pitfalls of mass media. It is designed to educate you and your children. The point of this education is media literacy. Being literate at the lowest common denominator means being able to read. But being literate in a more sophisticated sense of the word is to be empowered in how you deal with something. The same should be true with media. Media present us with an alternative reality that is always projecting an image or telling us, consciously or unconsciously, how to think and act. People who are media literate live their lives in mastery of media rather than it being, to some degree, master of them through its powerful persuasive appeal. Helping your kids become media literate is akin to giving your kids body armor against the influence of media. It makes them aware of the influence the media can have and therefore protects them against such influence.

Hopefully I have whetted your appetite. There are a lot of fascinating questions regarding the potential effect media have on your children. And there are a lot of ways you can help protect your kids from harmful media and teach them how to deal with lots of different types of media and mediated content. This book is a survival guide of sorts. I will tell you what the research finds, what it means to you, and how you can apply it in practice.

So now let's get started.

Babies and Toddlers

A FUNNY THING HAPPENED on our way back from the hospital. There we were, the typical proud parents, our first born in the back seat. The ordeal was over, and everyone was healthy and safe. We had read books, watched shows, gone to classes, and successfully delivered our first child into the world.

We were home.

We brought baby Aidan inside. He looked around a bit and, not really being able to focus anyway, decided on a little nap. Now what to do? We had no idea!

How anticlimactic.

So we did what any ordinary middle class family would do . . . we ordered pizza. Then we turned on the television and watched a movie. Sooner or later, the baby woke up, and that was it. TV, meet our son. Son, meet TV. You will surely have a very, very long and intimate relationship with each other, no matter how hard we might work to the contrary.

This chapter is about those first critical three years of life, and the introduction of electronic media to your children. As such, the question one asks is not as much the "what" question (that comes later), but the "when" question. When should my child start to watch? As we will see, the research thus far shows that to be a good parent you can work with television, if you use it smartly, even with children under the age of two. You should, however, try to minimize it to one half hour each day, or occasionally, an hour (see below for more information supporting this). Less is certainly better, but again, the important thing is not just how much you show your children, but what you show them.

With each chapter, the best place to start is to conduct an assessment of what you are doing with your child right now.

Baby and Toddler Self-Test of Media Consumption

1. My child watches television:
   a) not at all b) about _____ minutes or hours a day.
2. My child listens to music:
   a) not at all b) about _____ minutes or hours a day.
3. Yes or No: Although my child may or may not watch any television yet, the television is on adult programming while he or she is in the room.
4. Yes or No: My child has a television in her room.

So, how do you stack up? Put your answers next to the averages in the charts below (remember your answers to questions 3 and 4 for later on in the chapter):

Time Spent in a Typical Day, Zero to Three Years Old	
Listen to Music	1 hour, 8 minutes
Watch TV/DVDs	1 hour, 47 minutes
Does Your Child Three and Under Have a TV in His/Her Bedroom?	
No	30%
Yes	70%

Source: Kaiser Family Foundation

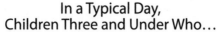

In a Typical Day, Children Three and Under Who...

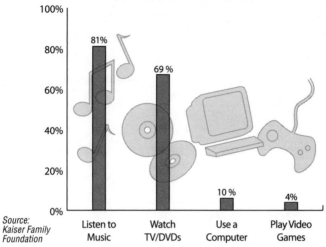

Source: Kaiser Family Foundation

- Listen to Music: 81%
- Watch TV/DVDs: 69%
- Use a Computer: 10%
- Play Video Games: 4%

Be honest with yourself. Are your children high media consumers for their age? Or low consumers? Or just average? Even if you are average, or slightly below average, read on, because many researchers have nevertheless found some impact that television has on your young child.

How Much Are They Already Watching?

As the charts on this page illustrate, on average, children ages two and under watch a significant amount of television (and remember from Chapter One, I define television as the use of television, whether it be for network channels, cable channels, or DVD/VCR viewing—in short, everything one uses a television for with the exception of video games or as a monitor for a computer). According to the Kaiser Family Foundation and other respected institutions, about three out of every four children under the age of two have watched at least some television in their short lifetime. Two thirds of all children watch just about every day. Of those who do watch just about every day, they watch, on average, just over two hours of television.

It is important to note that this average of two hours of television is, as discussed in the first chapter, one of those statistics where most watch less, because the average is being unduly influenced by the few who watch five or more hours a day.

TV Screens, Everywhere! Everywhere!

These days, there are so many more opportunities to watch a TV screen than was the case a generation ago. First off, families own more televisions, and on top of that, families also own computers capable of showing a DVD or other program. But additionally, we now take DVDs on the road. Today, many cars come with at least one DVD screen, and many other parents are buying portable DVD players, which now cost as little as one hundred dollars. I personally have two portable players, one for each boy! But we are very cognizant that the number of hours watching a TV screen is not just something that occurs at home. If one has to travel a half hour each way for preschool, for example, and the DVD player is on in both directions, you have just added an hour a day to your child's television watching. That is why we pull ours out of the closet only for long trips.

Though a kid might complain if they really want to watch and you disallow it, there is so much else to do in a car for local driving: Looking at the scenery, good conversation, and listening to music on the radio. So make DVD watching something that is only allowed on out-of-town trips, or in case of emergency (you know, those rare circumstances when it is a choice between total meltdown and the powerful distracting and calming effect of a short show).

But who are these people that let their kids watch six, even seven or more hours of television a day? Essentially, they are the children of households that have the TV on all day long. As the Kaiser study and other studies have found, children in such households are nearly twice as likely to start watching television before the age of one. And, such children watch, on average, at least a half hour more of television per day than households that do not have the television on habitually.

The heavy watchers of television also have televisions in their room. The Kaiser study also found that having a set in the bedroom, on average, contributes another 15 or so minutes per day of watching, though the numbers are again worse among heavy television viewing households. But even if you are not a heavy television watching household, this does not mean your children are completely safe from the effects of television. As we will see, moderate effects can come from moderate viewing. So whether you are a heavy or light television viewing house-hold, there is still plenty that needs to be reviewed below.

So now that we know a little bit about how much time kids today spend with media, what should we be worried about? And, as parents, how do we avoid the potential pitfalls of television viewing before the age of three?

Overall, researchers have been concerned with these issues:

1. When children should first be allowed to start watching television
2. Whether having the television on, in the background, has any impact
3. What is okay for children to watch at this age
4. Whether it is okay for a child to have a television in his or her bedroom

Let's go through each of these concerns one at a time.

When Should Your Child
Be Allowed to Start Watching?

Your child is screaming. She is holding onto your leg like a cat up a very tall tree, stuck. You promised yourself you would pay bills today . . . the seventh day in a row you've made such a promise. Now seems like a really, really good time to introduce your child to the television. A half hour right now of not having to deal with the child's needs would save your day, or better than that, save your sanity.

On one thing we can agree—we've all been there. And it's at this point where the soul searching often begins. The first question most parents ask themselves when it comes to exposing their children to mass media is: when? When is it okay to first turn on the TV and place the child front and center? The need often arrives at a predictable time: When parents reach a precipice, when household needs seem insurmountable. When it looks like everything is going to crumble before you.

Actually, if you are asking the "when" question, you're somewhat ahead of the crowd. Many parents just start exposing their children to television from day one without thinking about it. In fact, by a child's first birthday, as many as two out of every five parents already have a television in their child's bedroom, according to the Kaiser Family Foundation.

What can make the decision more difficult is the guilt from "peer pressure." The American Academy of Pediatrics somewhat famously (certainly the best press they ever received) proclaimed that children ages two and under should never watch television. Your parents may be giving you that not-so-subtle pressure to raise children more perfectly than they were able to do: No fast food, not too many toys! And of course, not too much television. Indeed, you may even have a friend that proudly proclaims that their children have not watched a second of TV and won't until they are five years old. Remember, that is probably the same friend who will say that their child can read by their third birthday. Don't worry, they can't. And they probably do watch TV, to some degree, as well.

It is true that there is a lot of research out there suggesting some potentially harmful effects of having your zero to three-year-old watching television. But it's not all bad. And none of the research finds much in the way of harmful effects for children who watch less than the average amount of television. So, your first job is to stop feeling bad about yourself. But beware, nevertheless: As much as television can help children learn, TV can also have negative effects on your children.

Of course, there may be some who choose to abide by the American Academy of Pediatrics' recommendation and forbid their zero to two-year-old from watching television. According to the Kaiser Family Foundation, about one of every five households reports that they are television-free in this age group. How about within more precise age groups? As the chart below shows, Americans are abiding by the AAP guidelines to a large extent, at least for the first year of life:

Children Who Watch TV

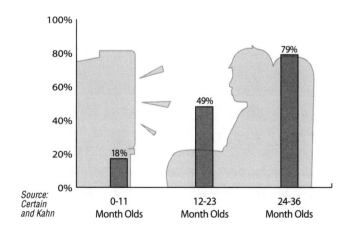

Source:
Certain
and Kahn

19

What this graph shows is that nearly four out of every five one-year-olds (or less) are not watching television. Good news indeed. About half of all one to two-year-olds is watching television, and four out of every five two to three-year-olds are watching television.

Importantly, there are factors that contribute to a greater likelihood of children under the age of two watching television. The more years of formal education of the parent, the less likely a child is to watch television. And as one might suspect, children of divorced parents are more likely to watch television, presumably because parents in one-parent households need more of a "break" to deal with chores and other tasks related to managing the home.

Of course, *if* there are positive benefits to high quality, educational television geared toward toddlers, then such households could be to some degree missing out. Nearly all parents who are asked about the effects they have witnessed from early television are far more likely to cite positive benefits than negative benefits. Many believe that television deserves to be part of the overall repertoire of learning experiences, and that small doses represent the optimal use of television for this age group. Indeed, while the AAP recommends no television under the age of two, the Canadian Paediatric Society recommends no more than a half hour a day before the age of two. Why the difference? The answer is that we actually don't really know where to draw the line. But it is thought that such a small daily dose of television does not place children in harm's way, while allowing for the possibility for learning. Still, it is worth noting that researchers have yet to figure out how to measure such learning (and as I will discuss, it may not even be possible to effectively measure the learning that might take place from television in the mind of a two-year-old).

Now: What about the other eighty percent of us who have allowed television viewing for our children ages zero to three? Public opinion surveys show that probably half of all children in this age group are watching, on average, an hour a day. One in five households is watching more than two hours. The table below shows exactly where your child might stack up to other American children:

How Does Your One-and-a-Half-Year-Old Stack Up?		
If Your Child Watches:	Kids Who Watch Less Than Your Child:	Kids Who Watch More Than Your Child:
One Hour or Less	43%	57%
1-2 Hours	58%	42%
2-3 Hours	72%	28%
3-4 Hours	78%	22%
4+ Hours	84%	16%

Source: Estimates based on Kaiser Family Foundation and other data

It is important to question the impact television watching could have on your children. In the sections below I will consider each of the major findings with regard to television at this early age.

So enough education on this issue, already: What is the bottom line, when should my kid start watching? On the one hand, you can follow the recommendation of the American Academy of Pediatrics and forbid television until your child is at least two years of age. Or, you can introduce television earlier, following the opinion of the Canadian Paediatric Society. Given what I review below, the research would suggest that watching moderate television starting on their first birthday, and perhaps even earlier, should be okay. However, read on, because you want to make sure you are exposing your children to the right kind of television.

Will TV Give My Kid Attention Deficit Disorder?

TV has been blamed for making us all have short attention spans. And if there is one study that has done more to buttress the position of the AAP, it is the finding that television has some link to Attentional Deficit and Hyperactivity Disorder (ADHD). In 2004, a group of scholars published research that was claimed by some to be the best evidence yet that the AAP was right in its advice that children under the age of two should be prohibited from watching television. These scholars purportedly found that exposure to television by children under the age of three led to subsequent attentional problems, including ADHD (Attention Deficit/Hyperactivity Disorder).

Specifically, they found that "a one standard deviation increase in the number of hours of television watched at age one is associated with a 28 percent increase in the probability of having attentional problems at age seven."

Don't tune out! I understand, most people do not really use these kinds of statistics in their everyday life. But whatever they mean, surely to most people, they sound pretty scary. But although scholars did find an undeniable relationship between television watching and attention problems, the likelihood of this happening to your child is quite small.

Statistics of the kind used by these scholars are quite difficult to whittle down to an easily digestible fact or number. One way to explain their finding is to use odds. Most people understand, for example, the odds of winning with regard to sporting events. For example if the odds are 2:1 that the New England Patriots will beat the Philadelphia Eagles, then the Patriots are twice as likely to beat the Eagles than the Eagles are to beat the Patriots.

Similarly, these scholars found that the odds of developing attention problems are 1.09 to 1 for every hour of television watched per day for a one-year-old. For three-year-olds, the odds were the same. What does this mean? Well, in their data, ten percent of children age seven was found to have attention problems. In other words, your child, regardless of television viewing, has on average a ten percent chance of developing attention problems. To round up the odds of 1.09 to 1 to the more digestible number of 1.1 to 1, that means that for every hour watched above the average daily consumption, your child's chances of developing attentional problems is ten percent greater than the average child. Ten percent greater than ten percent is eleven percent. Thus, simply put, for every one hour of television your child watches per day, the chance of actually developing attention problems increases by just one percent.

More recently, these researchers also explored whether violent television could be a leading player in the development of attention problems, instead of their earlier hypothesis that it was the total amount of television viewed. They found a more dramatic effect in this newer research: Each hour of violent television watched by preschool boys (there was no effect detected for girls) significantly increased the likelihood of developing attention problems by age seven. Remembering our baseline noted above that ten percent of children will develop some kind of attention problem by age seven, one might ask, what is the chance of developing such problems if one watches as much as three hours per day of violent television? The answer is, they have double the chance: twenty percent, or a one in five chance instead of a one in ten chance.

Interestingly, educational television was found to have no effect whatsoever on attention problems. All nonviolent television (educational or not) did have a moderate effect on boys. Thus, it is not the overall amount of watching, as earlier suspected, but the degree to which children watch noneducational television. And the data further show that as much as an hour of noneducation but also nonviolent programming will have no effect on the development of attention problems.

Therefore, if your child watches three or more hours per day, and the programming is not primarily educational, you definitely ought to consider whether the risks of your child developing attention problems outweigh whatever benefit you might attain from allowing your child to watch that amount of television. Even if the risk is small for your child, many would ask, is your child's health something you really want to put at any risk at all?

Well, okay, you say, I am not too worried my child will develop ADHD from watching television. But what about just a lack of an ability to stay focused in general? After all, again, television is widely blamed for giving us short attention spans, right? There is some mixed research out there on the general topic of attention span. In one basic experiment conducted by Friedrich and Stein, children were exposed to either *Mister Rogers' Neighborhood* or *Batman*. Those who watched *Batman* were found to have less tolerance for delay. In a study by Geist and Gibson, the effect of watching *Mister Rogers' Neighborhood* to the *Power Rangers* was compared. Children who watched the action-oriented *Power Rangers* were found to develop less patience on tasks they were asked to fulfill after viewing, while viewers of *Mister Rogers' Neighborhood* exhibited slightly higher levels of patience.

Other studies have looked at a different aspect of attention, for example, a lack of self-regulation—persistence in working on one task, the ability to control one's impulses, and the ability to tolerate having to wait for something. So far, few if any scholars have been able to link television viewing with any of these outcomes.

So overall, there is evidence that educational programs (like *Mister Rogers' Neighborhood*) likely have no impact on attention and patience, while action-oriented cartoons decrease attention and patience. As we will see in later chapters, it is not television watching in and of itself, but the watching of "empty programming" that can lead to poor behavior.

More specifically, however, scholars have noted that the one educational program most often used in these studies, *Mister Rogers' Neighborhood*, has one quality rarely seen now in most modern programming: the show occurs in real-time. There are no quick cuts and edits, flashing from one camera angle to another, from day to night, or scene to scene. Thus, many scholars actually think it is not whether programs are educational or not, but whether the pace of the program is in real-time or not. As such, parents should maximize programming that is filmed in "real-time" such as *Mister Rogers' Neighborhood*, *The Upside Down Show*, or *Blue's Clues*.

What Should My Child Watch?
(Or, Will *Baby Einstein* Make My Baby Smart?)

In three words, we don't know. Perhaps the more top-of-mind question to the average parent is, will *Baby Einstein* make my baby smart? The evidence is, as you might expect, we really do not know, and if we had to guess, the answer is no. One thing is certain: Babies seem to "like" these shows over and above any other kind of programming. But what do we mean by "like?" Here, "like" is defined as how much children look at the screen. Babies and toddlers tend to look at the screen more consistently when *Baby Einstein*-like programming is on.

So why do babies and toddlers like these shows? Because they have the perfect mix of just enough—but not too much—stimuli. Each scene in these shows is limited typically to one object, one area of focus. There is no cast of supporting characters. There are no subplots. There is no dialogue. What there is, however, is a consistent change of scene, from one solitary object to another. And importantly, the scene changes are perfectly timed, so that the typical baby or toddler gets a new look just about at the time when they are getting used to and potentially disinterested in the old scene. So there is a mix here of not too much stimuli, but at the same time, just the

Does Brainy Babies Actually Make My Kid Less Smart?

You might have heard the stories, as it was all over the papers for about a week in the middle of 2007: *Brainy Babies*, a popular baby and toddler DVD series, does not make your kid smart, according to research by Zimmerman and others. In fact, so the story goes, it could actually make them dumber.

Unfortunately, most articles revealed little about the details of the study. But these details, in this particular study, matter quite a bit: What these researchers found was a negative link between watching baby DVDs and video and language development. First off, this was only true among toddlers ages eight to sixteen months of age. There was no such relationship in children ages seventeen to twenty-four months (though no positive relationship either). Secondly, it seemed like every newspaper and Internet news article I read on this research claimed that the researchers found that DVDs specifically geared toward language development in babies and toddlers actually hurt language development. In fact, the scientists who conducted the research only asked parents how much their kids watched DVDs for babies and toddlers. And, these researchers note that most of these DVDs tend to not stress language at all. In fact, in many of them, language is close to nonexistent.

Indeed, it may be the case that such DVDs are bad for language development simply because, well, it is the last thing they stress: Unlike traditional older children's shows, there are no conversations, no dialogue, and very little vocabulary in such shows.

right amount, and at just the "right" pace. But it is important to note that in this case, "right" is defined as the pace most *liked* by children. Some argue that, like candy, this pace might be likable but may in fact have a link to attention problems later on down the road. But the link is still to date uncertain.

Another case in point is a study by Valkenburg and Vroone that compared the attention paid to various programming,

---

(continued)

Third, it is important to note that though they claim the effect between watching and poor language development is substantial, that is mostly in a specific mathematical sense. Overall, watching DVDs is a very, very small contributor (or lack thereof) to children's language development. The researcher's statistical models clearly show that a lot of other factors are much more important in language development, like reading to your kids, listening to music, etc. They also note that while one hour a day of watching these DVDs does suppress language development to a measurable degree, very few children are watching one hour a day of these types of shows. In fact, they found that on average, kids ages eight to seventeen months watch about fifteen minutes a day of such programming.

I am not saying we should not take this study to be an important one. The study clearly shows that yet again, it appears as if television is not appropriate for very young children, certainly children under one year of age. And perhaps, it also suggests that if you feel you have to find fifteen minutes here and there to get things done around the house, perhaps your best bet is a traditional children's television show like *Mister Rogers' Neighborhood* over these now-popular DVDs for babies.

specifically, *Teletubbies*, *Lion King II*, *Sesame Street*, and news and commercials aimed at an adult audience, based on the age of a child. The six to 18-month-olds clearly paid more attention to *Teletubbies* than any other program, while the most difficult program (not including news and commercials, which no child found particularly interesting), the *Lion King II*, best held the attention of the oldest children in the study (49–58 months). Interestingly, it was not the colors, laughter, child voices, and peculiar sounds that attracted babies to *Teletubbies*, since the researchers measured just about the same level of such features in the *Lion King II*. Rather, it was the pace and subsequent lack of complexity in presenting the elements that drove attention, meaning that *Teletubbies* differs from other programs in that the stories are presented with a slower-pace and less overlap between competing elements. In short, when there are characters and a storyline, the pace needs to be slow for babies and toddlers to maintain their attention.

So What Do They Learn, Anyway?

Scholars have long understood that a vast amount of learning in humans is done through modeling. In short, modeling is the simple action of watching someone do something, storing that information for later use, and at some later point in time, mimicking that behavior. The classic study regarding modeling has to be Albert Bandura's classic Bobo doll experiment, where researchers allowed children to watch adults hitting a life-sized Bobo doll with a mallet and then allowed the children to self-play, where the researchers witnessed the children enacting the same violent behavior they had just witnessed on the TV screen.

That experiment has been the flag-bearer for all those who decry the negative consequences of violence and television; certainly, the impact of violence is perhaps the most important concern we should have over what television teaches our children, especially as they become preteens and teenagers. But an important point lost in the flag-waving is this: Children don't just model violence from television, they model just about everything! And modeling is not the only method of learning children get from television, as a host of studies also show more direct cognitive learning about shapes, language, and other critical information.

But can two-year-olds model behavior from television? The studies have thus far been mixed. In one clear example of toddlers learning from television, Meltzoff showed that 14 and 24-month-old children who watch an actor pull apart a simple object and then put it back together, can then imitate such behavior. The level of success when watching a live person deconstruct and reconstruct an object versus watching the same thing on television were similar.

Is the World Inside the Television Our World or Some Other World?

Interestingly, children under the age of three tend to think that the world inside the television is not the same as the world we live in. Only at about the age of three do children start to realize that real people (as opposed to cartoons) in the television actually live in the same world they themselves live in. Unfortunately, this is also one potential reason children may start having nightmares, since they begin to believe monsters and other potentially fictional beings live in the real world along with real people! (See Chapter 2 for more.)

However, other studies like that of Schmitt and Young have found a more consistent trend where younger (19-24 months) children tend to learn better from a live instructor, while older children (36 months) are able to follow both live and televised instructors pretty equally. Then again, another group of studies found likewise results, but with "younger" children being defined as 12-15 months and "older" children 18 months and older.

More recent research suggests that the reason there are differences across studies with regard to babies and toddlers learning from television is that the direction given in the tasks embedded in such research may not be explicit enough. When children are given videos that speak directly to them, the programs are much better able to elicit a response. For example, if instead of just illustrating how to take a toy apart and put it back together, the actors on the video speak to the audience as they demonstrate such instructions, the viewer explicitly gains better results.

It might seem like quite a number of shows are using this strategy. *Dora the Explorer*, *Blue's Clues*, and many other shows often delay the "action" so that a character can face the camera and ask the audience member for help, provide them instruction, or otherwise get them involved. It appears such a strategy works, even with toddlers under two years of age.

In the end, it seems clear, despite a few studies to the contrary, that children over the age of one can learn from television. There is no evidence either way regarding children under the age of one. But just as children can model live behavior, children can model televised behavior, though they may need "additional" help from the characters on the television to make it clear that they (the characters) are speaking to them (your children) and encouraging them to think and learn.

A TV of Their Very Own

So your baby or toddler has a television in his or her room? Take it out. It does not belong in there! Some parents are quite surprised by the thought that someone would place a television in the bedroom of a newborn to three-year-old. Yet studies show that over thirty-one percent of children ages two to five in fact have a television in their rooms.

Link to Obesity

Research, such as studies by Dennison and colleagues, has shown that having a television in a child's room substantially increases the likelihood of that child being overweight. Specifically, having a television in a child's room increases the chance that that child's Body Mass Index will be in the eighty-five percent range or greater by about thirty-one percent.

Link to Sleep Irregularity

Like obesity, another outcome of television in children's rooms is potential sleep irregularity, though the link is moderate at best. And, it is important to note that "irregular sleep" is defined as the amount of consistency regarding when a child goes down for his nap and for the night, not whether the child has problems sleeping during the night.

The link between television viewing in the bedroom and irregular sleep can also be expressed through odds, and, strangely enough, the odds found by Thompson and Christakis are the same as with the attentional problems study: 1.09:1. Thus for every hour of television your child watches in his room, the chance that their naptime or bedtime is not consistent from night to night goes up by about ten percent. Given that about one-third of all children has irregular naptimes or bedtimes, this means that the increase in likelihood of having an irregular naptime or sleep-time is about three percent more per hour of television watched.

A final caveat concerning the results of this research is that sleep irregularity was defined by whether the parent of the child said "yes" to the question "is the child's bedtime/naptime usually the same from day to day?" The concern with this question is that it does not define the point at which a parent would define "the same." Put more clearly, imagine a child goes to sleep at 8:00, plus or minus about twenty minutes, every night. Does that cross the threshold of "usually the same" everyday? It likely depends on the parents' own perception and own definition of "the same." The point is this: Should we be concerned if watching television in the bedroom leads to some sleep irregularity, as defined in this study? The answer is at best unclear. If the example stated above (twenty minutes plus or minus) is considered irregular, then it is not likely something to be very concerned about, as there is no research showing any problems with allowing this small amount of leeway in your child's bedtime. If, however, irregularity was only noted by parents with a much greater range of bedtimes, say, two hours or more, then the link between television and sleeping warrants more concern. As of now, the data is very unclear as to whether parents should be concerned with the television-to-sleeping irregularity link. Parents should just be mindful of this link if they think their children's television habits are getting in the way of consistent and quality rest. Regardless, even this weak finding is yet another reason why it is not a good idea to have a television in your child's bedroom.

Most importantly, one of the strongest predictors of watching a lot of television is a child having a television in his or her bedroom. One of the real problems with a television in the bedroom is that bedroom television watching is largely unregulated, and noninteractive. Meaning, your child could change the channel (children around the age of three can develop this skill), and nevertheless, the child has no ability to ask for explanations if anything confuses them. And you as the parent will rarely "mediate," which is an academic term for co-viewing, where you interact with your child and help them learn from the television. As we will see in the next chapter, such parental mediation can drastically improve how much your child learns from television. There is, then, no easier way to limit your child's television time than eliminating the television from the bedroom.

Aww, How Cute! The Cell Phone as Toy

Little children LOVE cell phones. They see their parents talk on them all the time and there is nothing more interesting than pretending to do the same. But is it safe? There have been many substantial studies exploring the potential link between low levels of electromagnetic energy close to the head and cancer, headaches, and neurological disorders. Although nearly 100 studies have been authored on the subject, the majority are inconclusive, though some have suggestive findings of a potential link. But to date there is no conclusive evidence that cell phones, a primary producer of electromagnetic energy, especially energy emitted close to the head, cause cancer or other major ailments.

Still, it is thought that if there is a link, those most susceptible are children, and in fact, some studies suggest that the levels of electromagnetic energy in cell phones can actually "misfire" nerve synapses in a child's brain. As their brain is in a stage of maturation, this leads some to be concerned that children should not be exposed to such energy.

The safe bet is to disallow the use of cell phones by children under the age of seven. It is perhaps safe to allow kids to play with your phone so long as they are not on a call. If you want to be absolutely sure, turn off the phone before letting your kids play with it.

Music

There is a saying in the news media that "if it bleeds it leads," meaning, good news comes after a long list of bad news. You're probably not surprised, then, that when one considers the effect of the mass media on children, no one is talking about music. At least, not until they are teenagers and we start worrying about whether songs about "cop killers" and other ultraviolent acts become a potential hazard. For now, the good news: Music is good for you! At least, when you are zero to three years old. And in this case, "zero" literally means zero in the sense that you have yet to be born.

As you may know, music can be stimulating to unborn children. Hearing becomes possible around the sixth month of pregnancy, and studies show that musical perception occurs sometime just before birth.

After birth, children begin to imitate rhythm, words, and pitch by age three. In one amazing study by Tafuri and Villa, a group of mothers-to-be were involved in weekly music lessons during pregnancy, while a control group of mothers-to-be were given no such instruction. The music lessons involved singing as well as instrument playing. Amazingly, infant vocal-

Who Plays Music?

Three-fifths of families report playing music for their zero to two years olds on a daily basis, again according to the Kaiser Family Foundation, and the vast majority of those who do not play music every day still play music for an infant at least once a week. Parents with higher educational attainment play music more frequently, and parents under emotional distress play music with the least frequency.

izations recorded at two through eight months exhibited more structure in the children of the "music lessons mothers" than in the babies whose mothers did not take lessons. This included increased raising and lowering of vocal tones, distinguishable time intervals, and differential rhythms. While more research is needed, there are indications that early music leads to early musicality, that is, an understanding of music and the ability to better produce music of one's own.

Overall, just as with television, researchers have had a very hard time figuring out exactly what music can do to a baby or infant, simply because it is so difficult to measure music's potential effects on young children. But research has clearly shown that music is consistently rated as popular stimuli to children and that they are naturally inclined to learn music. Thus, music becomes a great learning vehicle. Toddlers may not know what they are saying, but surely, having a toddler learn to sing "Twinkle, Twinkle, Little Star" is a great first step toward future learning. And, a vast amount of research has underscored the ability of music to soothe, something every baby needs from time to time!

Conclusion: Strategies to Maintain a Healthy Electronic Household for Your Zero to Three-Year-Old

Do you need help? I can answer that in two simple questions. Does your child have a television in his or her room? Does he or she watch more than one hour a day? If the answer is yes to either of these, you ought to reconsider your child's media habits.

It's not easy. Why do people fail to reduce their child's television time, despite best intentions? In short, because they do not have a replacement. If one abruptly turns off the television on a child, what is going to happen? Likely, a lot of screaming. That is because when it comes to children, the most important lesson is distraction, distraction, distraction! If you have alternative stimuli other than the television at-the-ready, you will find the transition away from television easier.

So here is your homework for the weekend: When your child is napping or you find some other free time, spend an hour setting up fast "distraction attractions" for your child. These are objects and activities that are likely to divert your child's attention for a half hour or more. Then, when you find yourself putting your child in front of a TV, try one of these alternative approaches.

Distraction Attractions

Ye old kitchen. Take old kitchen objects and place them somewhere easily accessible. As is often the case, such objects are novel and interesting to a child under the age of three. When needed, pull one out. You'll be amazed how much time they will spend with just an old plastic spatula and an empty cereal box!

The old toy bin. Many families have too many toys. Between hand-me-downs and holiday gifts, many households have literally hundreds of toys, big and small. When you find your child intensely interested in a toy, allow him to play with it for a few days, then put it away for a month just as his interest starts to wane. Then, at that critical moment, say, when you are trying to make dinner and your child is hugging your leg and you are ready to turn on the TV, bring out that long-lost toy. If you have as many toys as my household does, you can repeat the strategy literally dozens of times!

The activity center. Do you have an activity center for your children? That is, a place they can color, paint, use chalk and the like? Every household needs one. Use this center strategically to minimize television use. For example, say your child starts each day watching television, and you want to break the habit. Simply set up a craft for the following morning before you go to bed. For example, cover the activity center table with paper and leave out some crayons or markers.

Families do not think of having their children do crafts because at that moment of high stress—when your child is screaming for something and you are busy doing ten other things—well, that is the worst moment for you to try to think of something for your child to do and then find the time to set it up. Get in the habit of preplanning these things. Look, your child is going to cry and scream tomorrow, at least, most kids age zero to three seem to with pretty regular frequency. So just as you go to the store to get more milk when you are running low, get the activities ready before you are in need.

The key here is to keep it basic. I am not suggesting you not interact with your child. Please do! I am only assuming you are likely the good average parent, meaning, you do interact with your child. You do arts and crafts with them, you play basic sports with them, you go to the park with them, to the library, and down the street on walks. But that is not when you need help. You need help when you have things to do. Pay bills. Make dinner. Have a conversation with your best friend from high school. Dress for work. These are the times of the day when interaction is simply impossible. We tend to allow our children to use television when we have no time. The trick is to have these readymade activities that a) take little of your time to set up and b) are quite likely to hold a toddler's attention for a good fifteen minutes to a half hour.

So get to it. Get that television out of the bedroom. Turn off the television when no one is watching, and turn off the adult programming (news, sitcoms, anything not specifically targeted for children) when the child is in the room. Play music for your child. And prepare a few simple activities and "toys" for easy access in times of need. The research does not indicate that being a good parent requires you to totally remove television from your child's life. You are just trying to minimize it to a half hour a day, occasionally, an hour. Less is probably better, on that there is little argument. But there is also little argument that the majority of families out there are probably exposing their children to more television than they should. So don't feel like a failure if, a half hour after reading this chapter, you find yourself allowing your two-year-old to watch the latest episode of *Teletubbies*. But do what you can to minimize exposure whenever possible.

CHAPTER 2 CHEAT SHEET

TELEVISION

DAILY DOSAGE	None if you can help it; at least hold out 6 months to 1 year and then only a half hour to an hour.
KEY CONCERNS	Potential stunting the development of the ability to focus.
REMEDY	Low consumption; "real-time" paced programming; interactive programming and interactive parenting.
COPING STRATEGY	Don't wait for it to happen: Pre-plan other distractions.

MUSIC

DAILY DOSAGE	As much as you'd like
KEY ADVANTAGE	Promoting development

CELL PHONES

USAGE WARNINGS	Be on the safe side: Don't let young children use them.

3

Preschoolers

WITNESSING A MOMENT of learning is something most of us have experienced. You beam with pride when you see your child unexpectedly learning something new. Hopefully, these moments are not uncommon to you, considering the joy they can bring. From ABCs to riding a bike, they are in part the gift of being a parent.

You most certainly have had more than one of these learning moments from television. Indeed, when asked if they have ever witnessed their child imitate positive behavior from television, nearly nine in ten parents said yes in a recent Kaiser Family Foundation study. Strikingly, only six in ten say they have witnessed negative behavior (and only one-third of parents of girls say they have witnessed television-related negative behavior). Over half of parents think television is a "very important" learning tool for their child's intellectual development (and the majority of others still think it is somewhat important). But of course, we do not want to judge whether television is "good for your child" just because, on balance, parents think so. We need to see what has been discovered scientifically. And most importantly, we need to understand *how* television can be a vehicle for learning, and how, conversely, it can sometimes be little more than a waste of time.

This chapter sets out to do just that. Preschool children age three through five are undoubtedly the most heavily researched of all any group, at least when it comes to television and learning. And, preschoolers are not just watching television. Over half have played a video game on a video game console that hooks up to a television set (though fewer than one in ten are using it on a typical day). At least seven out of ten have used a computer. And by age six, most children have been exposed to about 14,000 advertisements each year!

Preschoolers Self-Test of Media Consumption

1. My child watches _____ hours of television per day.

2. My child spends _____ hours on a computer each day.

3. I am _____ percent sure I fully understand what "educational" means with regard to educational programming: 0 to 50%, 50-75%, 75 to 90%, 90 to 100%.

4. Of the programming my child watches, _____ percent is educational: 0 to 50%, 50-75%, 75 to 90%, 90 to 100%.

5. I watch television WITH my preschooler, _____ percent of the time: 0 to 50%, 50-75%, 75 to 90%, 90 to 100%.

6. When I do watch television with my preschooler, I interact with him/her by talking about what is happening in the program, either during or after the program, _____ percent of the time: 0 to 50%, 50-75%, 75 to 90%, 90 to 100%.

The Average Preschooler

Preschoolers get into a lot of things. Painting. Dolls. Playing catch. Riding a bike. And of course, television, computers, and, to a lesser extent, video games. And just as a typical preschooler can often quickly pick up the gist of any age-appropriate puzzle or board game, they can also quite quickly pick up the skills needed to interact with electronic media. Two-thirds of four through six year olds can use a mouse on a computer. Over half use a computer without parental interaction. Nearly all of them by this point can turn the television on and off, and three out of four can even change the channels or load a DVD by themselves.

Generally speaking, television still tends to dominate electronic activities:

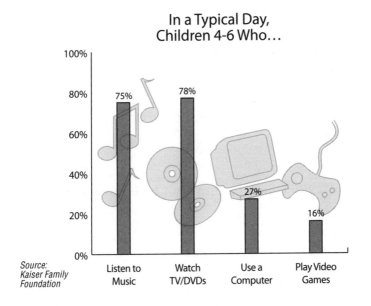

In a Typical Day, Children 4-6 Who…

Source:
Kaiser Family
Foundation

In fact, whereas zero to three year olds listened to music most often, television is now, for children ages four though six, the most frequent electronically mediated activity, as documented by Kaiser. And the use of computers and video games is up significantly.

Given this increase in media use, there are, at this age, many parents who create rules for their children's media consumption.

We need to remember that it takes quite a lot of brainpower to understand and fully interact with television, computers, and videogames. These media often involve color and sound with storylines and interactivity. Though some may have you think that children are nothing more than zombies wasting away in front of the "boob-tube," researchers do find that, in fact, by this age children achieve a high level of interactivity. Children pay more attention when there is action, funny or loud noises, or children on the screen. Even when they are not watching, they monitor the sound and refocus when some auditory signal suggests they should pay closer attention. Children tune into material that is comprehensible and disregard incomprehensible elements. As we will see later, this is quite important because parents who wish to encourage highly advanced educational television on their children might find their children choosing to tune out, simply because to them, it is incomprehensible.

Help! TV Is Going to Turn My Child Into a Zombie!

I think before we go any further on the topic of television and preschoolers, it is important to clear the air on any preconceptions one might have of the overall effect of television on young children. Forget about what show your child is watching: The question here is whether the very act of watching is having some terrible impact on one's own children.

A few well publicized books would have you think the answer is, absolutely! But beware of books with titles designed to scare you into buying them. The essential fact is that there is far more we do not know about television's effect on the very young than what we do know. That means that any writer on this topic must choose between only reporting what is known, or filling in the gaps in the research with their best guess or gut feeling. And, if a writer is convinced that television is having a terrible effect on our children, they tend to fill in the gaps with worst-case scenarios.

Moderate Effects

The majority of studies looking at relationships between television and its effect on your children suggest that those effects are, at best, moderate. Will television make your kid fat? Will television teach your child letters? Will television ruin your child's attention span? Will television show your child how to be a good citizen (what academics call "prosocial behavior")?

The answer for all these questions is, believe it or not, most likely no. Most likely no!? What is that supposed to mean? It means that, for example, when scientists conduct a study and find a link between television watching and being overweight among the very young, they do what any scientist would: They write a paper saying "television makes us overweight!" Writing such papers, after all, gets one published and furnishes notoriety. But remember this: Just because the scientists found a link does not mean you should necessarily care. In science, there is finding a link, and there is finding a *link*. The problem is that scientists tend to be so focused on finding the link itself that they don't stop to consider the real impact in plain, ordinary language.

So let's take an example. Will television make your three through five-year-old child overweight? Again, the scare-mongers like to tell you the answer is yes. But as we will see, the answer, for the vast number of children out there, is no. One hour of television watched per day has been linked essentially with a 1 percent increase in the chance that your child is overweight. The link exists, for sure, but should you really lose sleep over this? Certainly, parents have much more important things to worry about. That said, if your child is overweight or steadily becoming so, you should be asking yourself whether he is watching too much television. For the rest of us, we should probably be worrying about other, more important things that might have a negative impact on our children.

Brain-Drain Television?

So by now you are probably thinking you know the answer to the question implied at the top of this section "will the television turn my child into a zombie?" The answer is, again, most likely no. But some writers are convinced otherwise. Beware of things that "feel" right when dealing with science: Is that zombie-like watching of television telling us the watcher's brain has essentially gone into auto-pilot, or, conversely, does it mean that the brain is so focused at integrating the stimuli presented to them from the television that the outside world is temporarily taking a back seat? That is, is the television turning our children's brains off or on? Science really has yet to prove or disprove either position. But if you are already convinced that television is a terrible thing, the answer is all too clear! As a research scientist, I cannot go down that road. I cannot assume anything unless research supports that claim. Far, far too many bad decisions have been made in life because we feel we think we know the right answer, in the face of science that often strongly suggests otherwise.

The idea of "zombieism," the view of scholars who believe that television is destroying society, suggests that television offers us a high-paced, vastly more captivating television-world that makes us lose all interest in the real world. Why walk in the park when we can see such incredible nature experiences on television? Surely the park must seem boring by comparison? Unfortunately, these same researchers argue in the same breath that television is no substitute for real experience. Real experience is so much more interesting, as it is far more interactive, personal, and, well, real. That is why most studies show that television learning is never clearly superior to real-person learning.

So television sucks our interest away from the real life, *and* television doesn't even hold a candle to real life? I do not personally know of too many children who are not easily amazed by the outside world, regardless of what they see on television. So here is a case where, when research is lacking about whether television leads to "zombieism," where children just plain lose interest in the real world, writers who have a bone to pick with television find whatever anecdotal stories they can to support the negative view of television. That is not science, it is just one person's opinion.

These same writers equate television to a "sorcerer of old" who can cast a magic spell on us and make us pay complete attention to it over all other stimuli. What this argument forgets is that when someone encounters a wholly viewable experience, whether it is going to the zoo or watching a play, people tend to act the same way: All attention is paid to that which requires such attention.

So again, this argument of zombieism should either hold for all primarily viewable experiences, or should not be considered as evidence against any one viewable experience and not others.

These same writers also bemoan the fact that the television provides too much stimuli to children not ready to process it. Yet they also note that studies have shown that children very quickly adjust their response to stimuli based on expectations. That is, if they know something, like television, is going to present them with a high stimuli environment, they quickly lower their threshold to incoming stimuli to take in only as much as they wish. Again, both statements cannot be true at the same time. Regardless, as some of these writers even admit, quite a bit of children's television, including long-standing shows such as *Sesame Street*, have toned down the pace of their programming to better match the abilities of their young viewers.

In the end television viewing can no doubt have negative consequences on young children. However, research also shows that television can also have a positive effect as well. But most important of all, nearly every study shows that the impact of television is mostly dependent on one factor, and that is how much television children watch. Will your child turn into a zombie from watching television? The outlook is good, *if* she is watching five or more hours every day. What if your child is watching two or fewer hours per day? Here, the research strongly supports a "no" answer.

In the end, parents need to know their children, and come to know what television their children are regularly consuming. After all, the other irrefutable finding from all the research on children and television is that every child responds differently. Since you can only use the research as a guide to understanding a) if an effect is possible and b) if it is, how likely; your job is to base your judgment of whether television is affecting your child in a particular way based on this evidence *and* your own observations of your child watching television.

What Does TV Teach Our Children at this Age?

Perhaps the most important question in this chapter is, what is TV teaching my three to five-year-old? Although there is some evidence to the contrary, the short answer is, everything, though certainly not as effectively as we would wish.

There is much evidence suggesting that vocabularies can be expanded from television. In one experiment by Rice and Woodsmall, preschoolers were shown a 15 minute instructional television program that featured 20 novel words. Three-year-olds on average knew about 5.8 words before watching the program and 7.6 words after the program. For comparison purposes, a group of children were not shown the program, and as expected, their knowledge of the words did not change. The impact was greater for five-year-olds, who knew an average of six words before the program and 10.7 words after the program. So clearly, television can teach vocabulary.

Television vs. In-Person Learning

However, what was not clear from this experiment was whether in-person teaching would be more effective in the same amount of time. It is, after all, important to ask ourselves whether television can teach children better than in-person instruction. Most studies find that television is not as effective as in-person learning, though some have found somewhat equal levels of learning between the two. While television lacks the personal touch that many have found to be critical to learning, it does have the ability to use special effects, to move across time, to combine the visual with the vocal in a more exciting way. In the end, then, television may have an advantage (in a word, flashiness) and a major detriment (less interactivity and personal touch) compared to in-person learning.

From the available literature, it can certainly be said that television is not significantly *better* than in-person learning. Certainly, the literature seems to more often show that children learn from in-person learning more effectively than from television. For example, one pair of scholars conducted a range of experiments comparing videos to live learning.

Such research is typically conducted in a manner such as the following study by Meltzoff: Children are divided into two groups, the in-person group and the video group. In the in-person group, an experimenter plays with a puppet. This puppet had a mitten on its right hand and a bell inside the mitten. The experimenter would demonstrate putting the puppet on her hand, removing the mitten, and ringing the bell by shaking the mitten. The same actions were video-recorded so that those watching the video see nothing different than those watching someone demonstrate these behaviors live. Then, 24 hours later the children are given the puppet and experimenters measure how many of them will a) put the puppet on their hand, b) remove the mitten, and c) ring the bell. Generally, the

Teaching Girls to Be Girls

Sex-role stereotyping is something that many boys and girls learn at an early age. Most of this comes from parents. Parents who encourage their little girl to learn math and science are going to buck the stereotypical trend of raising a girl who has no interest in such "manly" pursuits. Parents who strongly admonish their little boy for crying because "boys don't cry" will tend to raise boys who hold in their feelings more than other boys. Others say some sex role development is pre-wired into boys and girls. Regardless of whether the development of such roles is due more to nature or to nurture, what is clear is that television can be a major player in the development of "gendered" identities and personalities. You are probably not surprised that scientists have found that girls who watch shows with fewer cues toward "traditional" gendered, stereotypical roles scored lower on tests designed to measure whether children know of these traditional gendered stereotypes. In short, there are programs out there (*Dora the Explorer*, for example) that buck the trend of typical gender stereotypes. If you want to minimize your children's exposure to such stereotypes, make sure they watch more of these types of shows.

children who witnessed such behaviors live are twice as likely to model and thus imitate some or all of these behaviors.

Importance of Interactivity

It is important to remember, though, that researchers have found that interactivity is a crucial part of any learning activity for preschoolers. It is likely, then, that the televised instructions on the puppet and mitten would have been more frequently imitated if the person on the television was more directly interacting with those who were watching.

Still, if one had to choose, in-person learning would be the favored choice. When parents are unable to provide in-person learning, television can be a second-best substitute. But beware: not all television is created equally. As we will see shortly, some programming is far more effective than others.

Television and Imagination

There is much more that television provides our children other than learning. Perhaps the second most researched area in addition to learning is the impact of television on imagination. Again, there are the arguments in favor and against a positive impact of television on the imagination. On the one hand, television exposes children to much that they probably will not witness in person (or at least, very infrequently). For example, a child may see a helicopter take off on television, but the chances of witnessing such an event firsthand, before the age of five, are slim. Television might spur the imagination with ideas modeled from the viewing experience, such as imaginative play about helicopters. On the other hand, some people argue that television takes time away from imaginative play, causing children to spend less time fostering their own imagination since hours are sucked away from playtime and put toward television viewing.

Most studies have found a positive impact of television on imaginative play. When it comes to the imagination, it matters which shows one allows one's children to watch. Shows containing a lot of action and violence have been found to have no impact on imaginative play, while shows with less action and little violence have a positive effect on imaginative play.

In one study by Singer and Singer, a group of children were shown episodes of *Mister Rogers' Neighborhood* while another group spent the same amount of time with an adult doing open-ended group play activities. Interestingly, the group that watched *Mister Rogers' Neighborhood* exhibited substantially more imaginative play in later play sessions than the group of children who played with an adult. However, a third group of children watched *Mister Rogers' Neighborhood* with an adult who actively pointed out specific events and elements the program exhibited, and these children exhibited the most imaginative play of all.

A different study suggested that programs that are slower-paced may more significantly boost imagination, as well as some other measures such as concentration, in comparison to fast-paced programs. Also, the same study found that the impact of television on imaginative play is more pronounced amongst children who were initially found to be low in imaginative tendencies before the experiment.

In short, studies suggest that television can have a positive impact on imaginative play. But again, this is only true for certain types of programming, is more true for some children than others, and is especially true for children who watch shows interactively with their parents. As parents, we are never off the hook!

TV and Prosocial Behavior

A final area of research on educational effects of television on children concerns what researchers like to call "prosocial behavior." This includes increased altruism, social interaction, as well as a lack of aggression and stereotypical attitudes toward others. In a review of nineteen research projects testing for a relationship between television and prosocial behavior, Mares and Woodard found that eighteen of the research projects documented a positive link between television and all aspects of prosocial behavior with the exception of aggression, which did not *diminish* with the viewing of prosocial behavior. In other words, in study after study, researchers have found short-term boosts in prosocial behavior for children who watched programming that underscored prosocial behavior.

What Programs Are Good for Children?

With the proliferation of 24-hour children's programming via Nickelodeon, PBS Sprout, Noggin, Disney channels, and other stations, it is of substantial concern whether all programming is created equally. It is not. Generally, programming that is designed to be educational first and entertaining second has a significant leg up on programming primarily designed to entertain.

Instructional Shows Versus Cartoons (and What Do You Do When You Can't Tell the Difference)

Much of the available research on the impact of television compares educational programming to cartoons or other action-oriented programming. As mentioned in Chapter 1, watching educational shows, like *Mister Rogers' Neighborhood* had no effect on a child's patience while watching the *Mighty Morphin Power Rangers* significantly lowered patience. And, as previously mentioned, educational programs have been found to have a positive impact on imaginative play, but cartoons were conversely found to have a negative impact on creativity and imaginative play.

Certainly, it can be difficult for parents not to cave in when children prefer watching flashier programs to educational programming. But here the evidence is clear: Parents should make sure that the lion's share of programming watched by their children is educational. When given the option of watching educational television or no television, children will almost inevitably choose the educational television.

But what is educational television anyway? Aren't some cartoons educational? Certainly. But there are others that are not. Ultimately, parents need to know the content of the shows their children are watching and decide for themselves. Educational programs *will* make obvious attempts to teach children some knowledge, be it vocabulary, thinking skills, counting, etc, while entertainment programs will be dominated by the story line and flashy visuals. This is the litmus test for whether a program is educational: There must be obvious and frequent attempts by the show to teach prosocial behavior, foster the imagination, or instruct children on letters, words, and the world.

Lucky for you, researchers have already done the work to determine whether some programs are educational or not. Such scholars have also delved into the question of what such programs can specifically teach children. These are described in the following sections.

Sesame Street

There has certainly been no program that has garnered more attention with regard to its effects on toddlers and preschoolers than *Sesame Street*. This now classic show has a particular focus on ethnic diversity. Because of this show's wide influence, scholars have also explored whether this has had any effect on children.

In one experiment conducted by the *Sesame Street* research group, a group of children were shown episodes of *Sesame Street* with either a racial mix of child actors or entirely ethnic minority child actors. Another group watched the same version of *Sesame Street*, though in this second version the child actors were all Caucasian. The children were then asked to point to pictures of children and asked if they would like to play with them. Those that watched the ethnically diverse version of *Sesame Street* picked a picture of a non-white child around 70 percent of the time, compared to children who watched the white-only version of *Sesame Street*, who only chose a non-white photograph 33 percent of the time. This study strongly suggests that watching television that contains ethnically diverse characters instills more open attitudes toward other people of other ethnicities.

There have been many other studies on the effects of *Sesame Street*, and the vast majority of them have found the show to have a positive impact. In one study by Rice and others, watching *Sesame Street* was found to increase letter recognition, body part recognition, recognition of forms, and sorting and classification skills, for example.

The impact of *Sesame Street* has been particularly studied with regard to disadvantaged children, such as the research by Paulson. This research found a link between watching *Sesame Street* and spending time reading rather than doing other activities. The same study found significant differences between viewers and nonviewers of the program, with viewers scoring much higher on tests of math, vocabulary, and school readiness.

Teachers take notice: In studies where teachers test students' school readiness, children who watch *Sesame Street* are regularly found to be more prepared. Long-term studies by the Educational Testing Service and other researchers have even found that watching *Sesame Street* five days a week during one's childhood translates into as much as a ⅓ of a letter grade improvement in many classes in high school (most notably, this was true more so for boys than girls). Teenagers who watched *Sesame Street* as a child also reported more time spent reading, had a higher academic self-esteem, and placed a higher value on academic performance than teenagers who did not watch *Sesame Street* as a child on a regular basis.

But the positive research does not end there. Many scholars have looked not at educational attainment but at a possible link between watching *Sesame Street* and prosocial behavior and general social development.

With regard to the issue of cooperative play (play in which children enact solutions to problems that include working together with other children or sharing) the evidence is mixed. While most research has found a link between watching *Sesame Street* and increased cooperative play, the link has usually been limited to tasks that the experimenters ask the children to conduct right after viewing, and such tasks have been similar to tasks seen on the program. Very little of the research has found the same sort of cooperative behavior when observing children later in general free play.

From time to time, the writers of *Sesame Street* have written shows and organized seasons of shows over certain themes. In 1983, the character who played Mr. Hooper died and the program dedicated a show to his passing away. In 1988 and 1989, the writers decided to show the characters Maria and Luis fall in love, get married, and have a child. And finally,

What Shows Are Educational?

Although it is easy to think of children's programming as educational or noneducational, in practice, some educational shows are more overtly educational than others, some are equally entertainment and education, and some are far more entertainment than educational. Unfortunately, good lists of educational shows are few and far between. The national organization CommonsenseMedia.org is a group of parents, educators, and media executives that does a fairly good job at determining what shows for children are educational. Here is their 2007 list for children ages four and under:

Reading Rainbow
Oobi
Mister Rogers' Neighborhood
WordWorld
Super WHY!
Play with Me Sesame
Pinky Dinky Doo
Mickey Mouse Clubhouse
Jack's Big Music Show
Barney & Friends
Dragon Tales
Between the Lions
Sesame Street
Signing Time
Mama Mirabelle's Home Movies
Franny's Feet
Mustard Pancakes
Backyard Habitat
Wilbur
Hip Hop Harry

As I urge elsewhere in this book, be sure you watch each of these shows at least once for yourself to determine its specific appropriateness to your child. Certainly, even in the list above, some shows are much more advanced than others, and parents need to make a judgment call on whether their three-year-old is ready for any one show.

starting in 1989 the show launched a four-year curriculum on race relations. In all subsequent studies on these topics by the *Sesame Street* research team, it was shown that viewers of *Sesame Street* gained significant knowledge and gained the right messages about these topics from the program.

Blue's Clues

Blue's Clues is a program designed from the outset to empower and enact self-esteem in preschoolers, as well as to teach thinking skills and problem solving skills and prosocial behavior. Research illustrates that the show achieves these goals to some degree. Not only does significant learning take place from each show, but also, it appears that children learn the specific ways of thinking promoted by the show.

In one experiment by Anderson and others, researchers tested the ability of *Blue's Clues* watchers and nonwatchers to solve riddles. One of the main goals of the program is for children to solve a riddle—what the character Blue is thinking—via three clues. As might be expected, viewers of the program exhibited a 20 percent increase in riddle-solving ability, and that percent increased as one watched more *Blue's Clues* episodes. Similarly, these researchers also found the same increase in the ability to view an incomplete drawing of an object and still be able to name the object. While nonviewers correctly named thirteen drawings, viewers were able to name seventeen. Furthermore, watchers of *Blue's Clues* were better able to match pictures of one object to another related object based on some similarity among a range of available pictures.

Mister Rogers' Neighborhood

The venerable *Mister Rogers' Neighborhood* has been studied for a number of positive effects. Watching *Mister Rogers' Neigh-*

borhood has been linked with imaginative play and increased self-regulation. *Mister Rogers' Neighborhood* has been of particular interest to researchers of the development of the imagination, as the program is known to be slower-paced than other programs and encourages make-believe. Regardless of the root cause, the consensus is that *Mister Rogers' Neighborhood* does foster some imaginative play, and imagination overall, and the increases in imagination are most pronounced amongst children who are not particularly imaginative in the first place.

I Watch TV with My Children . . . Is That "Better" Than Letting Them Watch Alone?

Yes! As has been shown in a few of the studies mentioned already, including those by Walling and Warren, watching with your children—and interacting with your children and the television—makes a *significant* improvement in what children get out of television. Although it is to some degree unclear why this is the case, there are a few plausible explanations. First, much of what children see on television is for the "first time," and thus often requires someone to contextualize, or offer background and explanation, to whatever it is they are experiencing. Second, it is a basic fact of learning that repetition is critical, and through interaction you are providing a level of repetition for your child to "go over" what they just experienced.

Unfortunately, only about half of parents say they usually or always watch television with their child. Considering how much of a boon this can be to your children, it would be great if more parents consistently spent time with their children in front of the television.

Some studies have suggested that parental interaction can *more than double* the learning a child gains from television. And importantly, there are two aspects to this learning. Not only can you can help your child attain the goals educational television sets out to teach, from problem-solving to letters and numbers. But also you are there to contextualize behavior, thereby helping your child learn what acceptable and unacceptable behavior is.

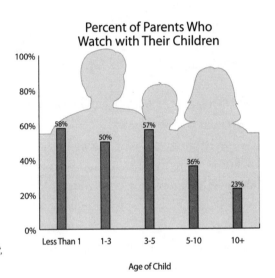

Percent of Parents Who Watch with Their Children

Source: Cheng, Brenner, Wright, Sachs, Moyer, and Rao

A number of media critics would argue that what is really going on is that somehow the interaction is personalizing the experience in a way that combats the tendency to zombieism noted earlier, that interacting keeps kids in a more alert frame of mind. There is no evidence that this is the case, however.

There is certainly nothing wrong, and a lot to be gained, by interacting with your child when she watches television. And not just for the child. Such events provide benefits for the parent as well as the child, in terms of gaining a stronger connection with your child and better understanding of how she thinks.

Aren't There Shows That Are Bad for Children?

It is important to understand that MOST shows are not appropriate for preschoolers. If the show is intended for an adult, then it is not intended for a child. Sure, there may be a few adult programs that might be "okay" for your child, such as the latest and greatest show on nature. But then again, are you ready for your three-year-old to watch lions eating dinner? So the safe bet is to keep the rule simple: If it is an adult show, it's not meant for your child.

Programming for teenagers and elementary school children should be equally avoided. These programs have themes

When I Watch with My Kid, What Should I Say?

The goal of parental mediation is to minimize the harmful effects of television and maximize the positive impact of television. And, you want to give your kid help for the things they need help in. Overall, scholar Robert Abelman suggests the following:

1. *What is Real and What is Not:* Letting your kids know that something is real facilitates learning about that object; and saying something does not really exist minimizes learning.
2. *Underscore Consequences:* Maximize the impact of rewards and punishment that occur on the television to maximize their imitation (for positive behavior) and inhibition (for negative behavior). This ensures that your child really understands just how good the good acts are and just how bad the bad acts are.
3. *Provide Motivations:* Talk to your child about why characters on television might have acted the way they did. Maximize the justifications for good acts, and discredit any justifications for bad acts.
4. *Verbalize Acceptability:* Let your kids know when you see something you would love for them to imitate, and let them know when you see something you would never let happen in your house.

that are too advanced for preschoolers. They also tend to contain much more cartoon violence and other unpunished negative behavior (remember, negative behavior is not necessarily a bad thing, so long as the program shows the perpetrators being quickly and harshly punished in some way). And remember what we stated in the previous chapter: Children do not get much from programs that are beyond their comprehension anyway. So there is no benefit to introducing them to more advanced programming.

At this early age, parents also need to be vigilant against programming that might be considered scary to preschoolers. This is actually one of the big dangers to exposing preschoolers to programming designed for early elementary children. Such programming is more likely to take on subjects like Halloween, or contain stories about monsters and the like.

Wouldn't Children Spend Their Time Better by Not Watching Television?

The short answer to this question is an unconditional "yes": Studies such as the one by Huston and others show that watching television, regardless of whether it is watched with parents or not, decreases the amount of time children under the age of five spend with the parents doing other tasks, as well as the amount of time children spend in "creative play," for example, drawing, coloring, playing pretend or dress-up, and playing with toys. Interestingly, it does not appear as if watching television decreases time spent in active play, that is, games involving physical activity.

Media critics will say that any time spent watching television is a waste because time is what is called "zero-sum," meaning you cannot make more of it, and what you have is all you get. While that is undoubtedly true, it is still important to remember that it is still very unclear just what might be gained and what might be lost by children who do one activity versus another. Certainly, there is a good argument here to make sure your child does not watch more than a moderate amount of television, because it is true that there is only so much time in a day. Each parent should question what else their child would be doing if he were not watching television. Writers who argue against television, at all costs, claim that television is clearly a second rate activity to creative play. This may be true, but presently it is unclear whether that statement is accurate. It may be that creative play and "good" (that is, interactive, educational) television offer different yet

How to Deal with Fright from Television

Kids can get frightened from many different things they might see on television and other media. Author Joanne Cantor provides a number of strategies to reduce fear in preschool children:

1. **A Hug:** Remember that fright is a physical reaction as much as an emotional reaction. And for children of this age, one of the best remedies is a physical remedy. Fright injects stress-raising hormones into the body. A hug help dispel these hormones. And the hug does not have to come from you. A child's older sibling or even having your child's favorite doll or other cuddly toy around can be useful for a good hug.
2. **Comfort food:** Yes, you don't want to use this one every time your child is scared. Save this one for when you really need it.
3. **Clearing the Room:** You have probably heard this one before, but that is only because it works. Check under the bed, the closet, etc. to clear the room of anything bad.
4. **Prevention:** As I have already mentioned, the best way to deal with fright is to prevent it by making sure your children does not watch anything inappropriate for their age.

still positive influences on a child. In the end, parents must assess their own child's daily schedules and make choices as to how their child spends their time. For children with a lot of creative play in their daily diet, the issue of television time displacement is less likely of a concern.

Will TV Make My Kid Fat, Even at this Early Age?

We already know that having a television in a child's room will moderately increase the chance of that child becoming overweight. But additionally, simply watching television, regardless of location, has been linked to being overweight in children, though the link is moderate at best, as shown by Gortmaker and others. As the graph below shows, this is really nothing to worry about unless your child is watching a substantial amount of television:

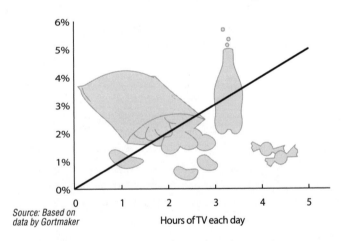

Percent Increase In Being Obese

Source: Based on data by Gortmaker

Hours of TV each day

As the graph illustrates, scientists have found a link between watching television amongst the very young and being overweight, but the impact is quite small. In fact, to round these numbers, there is only a one percent increase in the chance of your child being obese for each hour of television he watches.

10 Steps to Being a Good TV Parent for Your Three to Five-Year-Old

1. Know the Shows Your Child Watches

Understand the difference between an educational television program and "regular" children's programming. There are two problems with regard to defining programs as educational. First, many studies have shown that most parents are far, far too optimistic when thinking about which shows are educational. Scholars love to note that a majority of parents consider many game shows, interview shows such as *Oprah,* and even comedies like *The Simpsons* to be educational for their children. They are not! Consider ALL adult shows uneducational!

The second problem today is there are many programs that might be considered a little of both. Indeed, early studies were quite able to define their experiments as either "educational programming" or "cartoons." Today the line is not so clearly drawn. Many shows, including *Sesame Street,* have cartoon elements. And many cartoons, such as *Arthur* and *Curious George,* have noncartoon elements. Are *Arthur* and *Curious George* educational? Certainly, there is something to be gained by such programs. But just as certainly, these programs do not explicitly aim to teach children vocabulary, numbers, and the like. Still, they do attempt to teach prosocial behavior by example, and consistently provide consequences for bad behavior. The "easy days" are past, when there was a very limited number of children's programming and that programming seemed to be quite explicitly educational or not.

Does, for example, *Max and Ruby* teach inter- and intra-personal dynamics, as its introduction on the Noggin network claims? Well, think about it. If children learn through imitation, then any show that shows two characters interacting with each other will teach interpersonal dynamics.

So, how do parents decide? One solution is to limit children to viewing explicitly educational television only. For shows that do not have explicit educational elements, parents should make their judgment on three factors. First, is the vast majority of behavior exhibited by the characters of a show "model behavior"? And is there some sort of "punishment" for bad behavior? And secondly, can you detect within the story line lessons that, though they may not be explicitly "educational," still nevertheless seem to be on the right track? Finally, is the show age appropriate for your child? For a while, my three-year-old son was really interested in *Arthur*. But I often wondered what he got from it, since the characters are in elementary school. Their jokes are decidedly advanced for a three-year-old. I doubt he got any of them. And I am not quite sure I was ready for him to see "bad" children as some of the characters on the show can be. In the end, I decided to phase out his watching of the show. Overall, parents need to think about such questions, and make their best decisions based on the answers to those questions.

The final point to be made about educational television is that television has changed remarkably in the past few decades. That is, many of us can probably remember the six channels we had growing up, between network television and a few UHF channels. Today, there are so many choices. My first child has never really liked *Sesame Street*. If that were true when I was a kid, I would have lost about 25 percent of the educational programming available to me! In other words, there were only about four educational shows on when I was four years old. Today there are many options. He may hate *Sesame Street* but he loves *WordWorld*, *Super WHY*, and many other shows that are outright educational yet still perceived as cool by him.

2. Challenge Your Child, But Not Too Much

Children have a hunger to learn. And, children, like all of us, learn best through repetition. This means that the best pattern of viewing for your child is first an introduction of material that is new and challenging, followed by repeat-viewings over time of the same program. However, there are two important caveats. First, at a certain point the child should "get it," at which point you may find your child not paying attention anymore, or even asking you to watch something else. The program has ceased to be challenging to them and as such it no longer holds great interest. Second, do not initiate new programming to your child that is miles above her capability. This will even more quickly turn off a child, and potentially leave a negative feeling toward a show. Then, when the child is ready to handle that show, such pre-programmed disinterest must be overcome for them to regain interest. More importantly, there is some research indicating that watching shows that are too complex for a child to handle may have some negative impact on cognitive development. So challenge your child . . . but with shows you know they will be able to understand and, eventually, master.

3. Your Child Should NOT Have a Television in His or Her Own Room

Some parents claim the television is the only way their child goes to sleep. Other parents prefer the convenience of having their child have their TV time in their own room. Either way, the television should not be there. Your child will find a different way to fall asleep. Even though it might take a few nights of turmoil, teaching him to go to sleep on his own will only help him grow. And, I guarantee that once the television is out of his room, his their overall number of hours watching television should decrease as well.

4. Try to Take at Least Some Time during Your Child's "TV Time" to Interactively Watch Television with Her

Though scholars do not say as much, all evidence suggests that there is a great importance in you teaching your child how to watch television. That may seem a little odd, after all, all you do is turn it on and watch! But as will be discussed in later chapters, television has become our culture's primary story teller and children need their parents to tell them why the story teller said this or that. And in addition, the television is capable of showing so many different things, and often many at the same time. Undoubtedly your child sees much that she does not understand. You can be there to help her. Remember, interactivity is the most important element you can bring to the table to help your child learn from television.

5. Turn the Television Off When They're Not Watching

To date there is one area of research still grossly lacking in data, and thus was not discussed earlier in this chapter. The question is, is having the television on in the background a distraction to children? Does it impede their ability to concentrate? Certainly there is much anecdotal evidence to suggest that children will at least "watch with one eye" if the television is on, even if it is on for adult rather than children's programming. So while there is certainly a lack of understanding on how this might affect a child, the safe bet is to keep the television off while children are present as much as possible. This at the very least shows children that their parents have self-control, a very good behavior for them to model!

Most importantly, the best chance your child has to see something they should not is when the television is set to an adult program and left to play in the background. *Oprah* could be discussing the death of a parent, a topic far too advanced for three-year-olds. The typical beer commercial may show women with few clothes and men tackling each other to get at the women. The news can show all varieties of graphic violence. In short, there is a far greater likelihood that if the television is on, children will see something inappropriate. Make it a habit of turning the television set off when no one is watching, and only watch your shows when the children are in another room.

6. Too Much of a Good Thing Is Always Too Much

Children have lots they need to do every day: nap, play, learn, and interact. A moderate amount of television appears to potentially have some very beneficial effects (assuming of course that your child is watching the right programming), but too much of it does lead to a higher prevalence of negative consequences, from attention problems to obesity.

7. Review Your Child's Experience

Just as you might ask what your child did at preschool, you can ask your child what they watched, or better yet, learned, on television. This gives you an idea of what is important to them. Also, it gives you a chance to hear about something that was NOT good, something that you disapprove of them watching. From an educational standpoint, reviewing the television your child watched, assuming it was educational, allows for repetition, which, as you know at this point, has been shown to be critical for learning. In the end, being a good parent means being an involved parent, and just as a good parent asks what their child learned at school, so too a good parent can ask what their child learned from television. Finally, if you stress the learning element of television that establishes that television is an instrument of learning as much as it is an instrument for entertainment.

8. Remember, Every Child Is Different

Do not be too concerned if your three-year-old seems to be getting nothing out of *Sesame Street* or other educational programming. After all, the research all shows that the gains made by children with regard to these programs are much more pronounced among five-year-olds than among three-year-olds. What this means is that some three-year-olds probably do quite well with educational television, and others are not quite ready for it yet. There is no established link between "getting it" at this early age and future achievement. It might just be that your child is working on other things, or it may be that your child is getting it but doing so quietly. You don't need to force television on your child. There are, after all, plenty of other activities to do.

9. They Have to Ask Permission

One of the most basic ways to limit exposure to media is also one of the most basic: Make certain your children understand that they are not allowed to turn on the television or any other media without your permission.

10. Make Rules

The majority of parents have rules for watching television. Make rules that work for you and stick to them. These can include total time allowed watching, programs allowed, and how much time is allowed in one sitting. You can even make a rule for yourself that you'll have something planned for your children so that when TV time is over there is something else for them to move on to.

As this section has reviewed, television offers a lot of learning potential, and a lot of opportunity for abuse. But I hope it is clear that it is not necessary to throw the television out of the house to be a good parent. Rather, the goal should be to become its master. Use it wisely, moderately, and interactively, and you will maximize what your children get from it and minimize any potential hazards.

Computers and Internet

In a typical day, six percent of zero to three-year-olds use a computer, according to the Zero to Six Kaiser Family Foundation Study. But for four through six-year-olds, this number explodes to twenty-seven percent. And while only one-third of the younger group of children has ever used a computer, by age six, three out of four children have used one. Among those who do use a computer, four through six-year-olds are using it, on average, one hour a day.

Many four-year-olds are in fact using a computer every day, I was in junior high school the first time I sat down in front of my first Apple! Many parents find themselves clueless as to what it is like to be six and using a computer. (Just wait until we start talking about cell phones and iPods.) Indeed, computer use has increased significantly just in the past few years. A recent study found a twelve percent increase in the use of a mouse in two-year-olds (from five to seventeen percent) in just the past four years. In that same survey, at least ten percent of two-year-olds had gone to a website, but none of the six-year-olds in the study had ever gone to a website when they were age two.

Of course, since we have children that use computers for more than an hour a day, there are critics who are calling the use of computers by children "the end of childhood." Childhood is something you cannot get back, and computers, some say, are stealing it away.

Is there truth to this claim? To date there is very little research on the use of computers by four to six-year-olds. The available research shows that children of this age can learn quite a bit from computers. Nevertheless, the concerns raised by authors who bemoan the rise of computer use by children are valid, if only for the worst offenders.

It is important to note that while the vast majority of four to six-year-olds are just starting to dabble at the computer, it is still worth noting that that one quarter of these children are using a computer just about every day, and for an hour on average. So again, we have the same problem as we explored with television. It appears about one in ten children are using a computer over an hour, everyday. Although it is unclear if heavy users at age five turn into heavy users at age fifteen, it certainly seems likely. So again, there are families who should certainly be concerned with their daily diet of media, this time, regarding computers.

There are no clear guidelines for computer use at this age. But a fair measure to all, I think, would be to find a place where positive learning is maximized, potential negative effects are avoided, and far more time in the day is left to play with siblings and peers and to interact with parents. Thus, to get an idea of what is the right amount of time, we first have to understand the potential positive and negative effects of computer use. Overall, the complaints about computers and childhood are as follows:

1. *Physical Hazards:* Musculoskeletal injuries and visual strain due to long hours at the keyboard and monitor, as well as obesity from having a sedentary lifestyle.
2. *Emotional Impact:* Heavy use of computers, critics claim, can lead to a lack of self-discipline and self-motivation, as well as emotional detachment from one's community.
3. *Limiting Social Connectivity:* Using computers could lead to social isolation.
4. *Intellectual Pitfalls:* These include lack of creativity, stunted imaginations, sub par language and literacy skills, problems being able to concentrate, and lack of patience.
5. *Moral Corruption:* This includes exposure to violence, bigotry and pornography, and exposure to information that is lacking moral content.

Do these criticisms of computer use have any merit? The authors of *Fool's Gold*, the book where many of the complaints originated, provide many assertions from a panel of doctors and other "elites," but the volume of actual scientific research they provide to support their claims is quite limited. Still, I reviewed the research and did find that some of these concerns have scientific merit. Certainly, it is possible for any child to suffer from any of the maladies that are noted above. That cannot be denied. But are any of the problems noted above so prevalent as to warrant the concern of most parents?

Physical Impact of Computer Use
Critics claim that it is "virtually impossible" for computers to be set up ergonomically for children, and cite a number of exemplars of people who have had significant physical problems due to heavy computer use. As adults, we are probably quite used to hearing about the potential problems of

computer overuse. Most large companies will at some time post guidelines on proper posture. Most doctors recommend walking around ten minutes each hour during heavy computer use. And no doubt, cases of carpal tunnel syndrome and other repetitive strain injuries have gone through the roof in recent years.

But unfortunately, there is little research on the physical impact of heavy computer use on children. Indeed, it would be hard and unfair to do so (imagine taking one hundred children where fifty get to play outside for four hours straight, for a week, and the other fifty have to type for the same amount of time!). What is known is that bad posture can lead to musculoskeletal problems in adults. And studies have found that most computer workstations are not sized appropriately for

Design Your Computer Workspace to Fit Your Child

Designing a computer workspace for a child follows the same guidelines as setting up a computer workspace for an adult. Here are a few easy guidelines:

- Feet on the floor, back upright, with back support, elbows at ninety degrees. This is standard ergonomics, and requires a smaller table and kid-sized chair.
- Monitor should be eye-level, about 18 to 30 inches away. Adult keyboards are quite large for a kid, though at age three to five, most computer activities will not be keyboard intensive. Finally, try a trackball instead of a mouse, as they are much easier for children to operate.
- Children's feet do not have to reach the floor, just something solid, like a footrest or even a stack of telephone books. A sofa pillow or rolled-up pillows can be used to provide back support.

children. Thus, children who use a computer for even a moderate amount of time may be in greater risk simply because they are trying to work in an adult-sized workspace.

That said, as of 2002 there have been no studies that have scientifically linked computer use in children to any physical disorders, though it is still likely that overuse increases the risk, as heavy use of computers has been shown to be associated with pain and discomfort in college students.

Emotional Impact

Does computer use lead to a lack of self-discipline and self-motivation, as well as emotional detachment from one's community? In a word, no. Can extremely heavy use be a contributor to these outcomes? It is likely. Then again, the same might be said for just the opposite—that persons who tend toward isolationism and emotional detachment will get hooked to heavy computer use. But again, to date, there is nothing in the literature showing a causal (scientific) connection between computer use and these outcomes. Indeed, during the preschool years, computer use is often child-motivated, meaning it is not the parents that are pushing their children toward computer use but the kids themselves who want to get on a computer. This seems to me a certain type of self-motivation, not lack thereof.

Limited Social Connectivity

This much is clear: At this early age, if your child is spending an hour every day using the computer, approximately half of that time is spent playing outside amongst lighter computer users. There are so many hours in the day, after all. Whether an extra half hour outside is a concern is pretty much up to the parent. Children who get four hours a day playing outside are not likely to be greatly impacted by losing an extra half hour.

But if your child only spends an hour or so playing, then an hour of computer use seems, on balance, too much.

As for later years, as we will discuss, computer use has ironically been shown to increase social connectivity in many ways, from the number of persons one interacts with to the amount of time children spend "talking" (in person or via instant messenger or e-mail) to friends.

Intellectual Pitfalls

So computers lead to a lack of creativity, stunted imaginations, sub par language and literacy skills, problems being able to concentrate, and lack of patience, at least, according to its critics. Unfortunately, these claims are based on the usual nonscientific opinions of a select number of people. "Unfortunately," admits one critic from the *Alliance for Childhood*, a group of concerned professionals whose goal is to restore creative play in children, "almost no research has been conducted on the potential for computers to stifle children's creativity and imagination." Instead, critics fall into this "it must be true" trap. The argument goes like this: Media does all the imagining for your child, so there is nothing left for your child to imagine. It sounds great, I admit, and there is probably a kernel of truth to it. Indeed, as a musician throughout most of my teenage years, I used to not want to watch music videos because I preferred having my own images of what a song meant to me.

On the other hand, there is an alternative argument, and that argument is that the imaginations of children are limitless. After watching a show where a helicopter rescued a person who was stuck on a cliff, my son decided he would "save the dinosaurs" by airlifting them via helicopter. This he proceeded to do with his toys. The point is, children often take what is given to them and "take off" from there (pardon the pun). Just because computers and television offer a more richly and specifically defined vision of things (compared to, for example, books) does not necessarily mean that all the imagining is done for them. It might just give them more information to feed into their imaginations.

Computer Non Sequiturs

Another odd argument for those critical of computers is that computers, like television, ruin children's sense of wonder about the real world. This is a rather simplistic notion that "they have seen it all on television or computers," so why go out there and actually see it?

Please. Not only is there not a shred of evidence to suggest such an effect, television and computers can often serve as the catalyst to actually go out there and see it for oneself. For every one child who might say "no" to going to the zoo because they "saw it all already," there are likely many more whose excitement is evermore intensified to see animals up close and personal because their appetite has been whetted by media.

Yet another odd argument is the blanket claim of computers stunting language development. The crux of this argument is as follows: Language is most effectively developed through verbal interaction with others. If one spends all day in front of a computer, how can one interact with others? Certainly, there is no arguing with this statement. But it presumes that 100 percent of the time spent in front of a computer is time that otherwise would be spent in conversation with others. Instead, studies that attempt to figure out what is being "replaced" by computer-time find it to be a mix of playing outside, reading, and listening to music. And while I personally would prefer my kids play outside, read, and listen to music, the argument that computers stunt language development does not hold water because computer use does not "replace" verbal interaction with others.

Of course, this argument ignores educational software designed to teach language development and math development. When computers are used well, they teach. Studies like those by Li and Atkins and others show improvements in language development, spatial representation, visual attention, math skills, and overall academic achievement. Amongst preschoolers, early computer exposure was found to be linked to faster understanding of preschool-level concepts and cognition. In short, computers can effectively teach preschoolers the lessons they need to learn at this age, and prepare their minds for learning in kindergarten and beyond.

So How Do I Help My Child Use Computers the Right Way?

That computers can teach is unquestioned. What is questioned, however, is whether they can do so better than live instruction. In one study, it was found that computers did a poorer job than teachers in teaching numbers to children, specifically those children who had little or no mastery of numbers. But interestingly, children who had initial familiarity with numbers in fact learned faster from computer instruction than from teachers.

It has been shown that software and computers themselves serve as better teachers when they are designed specifically for young children. This includes visual cues to link the results on the monitor to actions on the keyboard and using meaningful instructional graphics. Studies show that little changes can make a difference in the amount of learning children gain from computers, as less of their effort is spent just trying to make things work. What are the key areas parents should focus on when it comes to their children using a computer a home? Longtime researcher on computers and children, Susan Haugland, finds five areas. They are:

1. Software selection
2. Computer time
3. Internet use
4. Family interaction
5. Supervision

Software Selection

If there is one clear problem with computers and children, it is that the vast majority of software being used by children is not considered educational. And even if present in the home, educational software tends to be under-utilized, if at all.

There are two broad categories of educational software. "Drill and practice" software is designed to test kids on specific skills. "Discovery-based" software is still educational, but in the context of a game-like setting or other more open-ended architecture. The latter has been shown to be much more valuable to learning at this age. These programs encourage kids to solve problems without pushing them to do so. They make computers more interactive and fun. And as such they are more able to enhance learning.

Computer Time

Just as with television, you should set guidelines on computer use. At this age, an hour a day is probably too much. But the time spent on the computer should rightly vary by how much you are interacting with them and providing them educational software. If your household only has two software programs useful to a five-year-old child, you should probably not have them on the computer consistently for a long time. The goal here is to constantly cycle through two stages: First, challenging them with new software, and second, allowing

Educational Software

CommonsenseMedia.org provides a good list of educational software. Below are the most highly rated games by age:

AGES 2 AND UP
- Giggles Computer Funtime for Baby: Shapes

AGES 3 AND UP
- Finding Nemo: Learning with Nemo

AGES 4 AND UP
- Miss Spider's Scavenger Hunt
- Reader Rabbit Reading Learning System
- Clifford Phonics
- Rescue Heroes Mission Select
- Little Bill Thinks Big
- Didi & Ditto Kindergarten

AGES 5 AND UP
- Hearing Music
- Mia: The Kidnap Caper
- Dragon Tales: Learn & Fly with Dragons

AGES 6 AND UP
- Puzzle Play Software
- I Spy Mystery/Fantasy
- Didi & Ditto First Grade: The Wolf King
- Reader Rabbit 1st Grade Learning System
- I Spy Spooky Mansion Deluxe
- JumpStart Study Helpers Math Booster

them time to master it. But even if your child is voraciously taking on every challenge you give to them, there is a limit at which they will get fatigued, where you should start to worry about physical discomfort.

Another concern in this regard is starting to think about total "screen time," including video games, computers and television. If your child uses a computer for an hour a day and television not at all, that is very different than using three hours cumulatively between all electronic media. You want your children to enjoy and learn from each medium, but not to the extent that they are spending three hours a day between the computer, video games, and television. As much as computers are a great vehicle for learning, so too is unstructured play outside, and imaginative play inside. Make sure your child has a "balanced" diet of activities throughout the day.

Internet Use

Internet use? Am I to allow my four year old to browse the Internet? Of course not. And even if you allowed it, a four year old would, geniuses aside, not have any idea how to do it.

But the Internet presents a wealth of resources for your child to learn. Try this as an interesting exercise: ask your child about something they like, or something they want to see or learn more about. Whatever the answer is, type it into a popular web search engine and spend fifteen minutes exploring what you find. The possibilities are endless. Animals, trucks, make-believe creatures, or even activities like painting and puzzles. It is an opportunity not just for your child to learn, but also for you to do it interactively with your child, and to also teach your child a little about the joy of learning and discovery.

Family Interaction and Supervision

One of the beauties of child interaction with computers at this early age is that there is not much your children can initially do themselves. They need you to teach them how to use a mouse and keyboard, and then, how to play each computer game. So at this age, computers are actually an excellent vehicle to foster family interaction.

Advertising

Finally, a topic we can all agree on! Nothing makes a child grow and develop like advertising. The more, the better.

If that were the case, then Ivy League schools would be inundated with child geniuses wanting early admission. Unfortunately, children and advertising share a shaky relationship. Even if your preschooler has never watched an hour of television, he or she is likely to have been exposed to thousands of ads. For those who do watch television, the average two to seven-year-olds consume seventeen minutes of advertisements each day.

Do Preschoolers Know What Ads Are?

Kids know ads. Children do notice that something different is happening on the television. According to a number of studies including those by Levin and colleagues, as much as eighty percent of four and five year olds correctly identify commercials as distinct and separate from the regular program. When shown different clips from both commercials and programs, the majority of three-, four-, and five-year-olds were able to correctly identify commercials as commercials and programs as programs. This is not to say that they understand that commercials have a different intent than programs. It is rather difficult to measure whether children ages three through five understand that commercials are designed to encourage them to buy things, but some cutting-edge studies like those by Donohue and other are finding that many three to five-year-olds understand this function.

In one study by Donohue and others, researchers found a commercial for Fruit Loops that aired in 1972. The ad was especially attractive to the researchers because there is never any suggestion in the ad that children try to acquire the product, or ask the parents for the product. Nevertheless, children were asked "what does Toucan Sam want you to do?" and provided two pictures to choose from to answer the question. The first picture showed a mother taking a box of Fruit Loops off the supermarket shelf, the second showed a child watching a television screen. Nearly all six-year-olds and three out of four two to three-year-olds picked the first picture. However, it is not clear to me that this study was really a fair test of advertising intent. And a replication of the study that

What a Cast of Characters!

Tony the Tiger. Ronald McDonald. Diggum. And of course, Scooby Doo and a hundred other television characters. Why so many characters? Because they work. Not only do these characters ensure that children will recognize products when they see them in the store, they actually greatly assist preschoolers to be able to remember the product even when they don't see it. Thus having such colorful characters associated with products ensures that children will ask their parents for that product before they even step foot in the store.

attempted to make the test more difficult with a four picture selection scheme found no support whatsoever that the children understood intent. But it suggests that preschoolers do understand that ads are telling them to buy things. Most studies find this to be true at least of five-year-olds, if not younger children as well.

Similarly, the majority of five-year-olds understands the disclaimers in ads, such as, "part of a nutritious breakfast" and "each sold separately." But few three-year-olds comprehend what these statements mean.

Do Ads Work?

Advertising works on children. Preschool age children clearly respond to both the audio and visual elements of advertisements. Ads tend to show the actual product in advertisements, so that children will recall the ad when they see the product in the store. But even more so, children remember the class of product in advertising, such that they are more likely to request, for example, cereal for some time after seeing a cereal commercial. Research has also underscored the obvious, that children will actively and repeatedly attempt to persuade their parents to buy brands they have seen in advertisements.

Advertisements persuade children. There are countless examples of this phenomenon. Some prey on the desires of younger children to be older, if even just a few years older. A four year old wants to be five, or even six or seven. No matter how hard we try to explain, kids always seem to want to grow up faster than they actually are. And, sure enough, research by Stoneman and Brody on advertising to preschoolers shows that ads that have models that are a few years older than the preschoolers themselves are far more persuasive than the same ads with models their own age, and far more effective than ads with younger models.

Whether children understand the persuasive nature of advertising, that is, how ads specifically "push their buttons" to get them to buy things, is not clearly understood. But most studies have failed to find any evidence to suggest that children under eight years old understand this underlying goal of advertising.

Researchers Pine and Nash compared letters written to Santa by children with heavy media exposure to those written by children with light media exposure. They found in three to four-year-olds that the children who were exposed to a lot of media made more requests to Santa, and more of the requests were of brand-name products. In short, ads work: even at age three, children start to learn to want things, and to ask their parents (and Santa) for them.

As this chapter has illustrated, the media is a tool that can be utilized to great success or misused to significant detriment. The key is of course oversight:

- Know what your children consume
- Moderate their exposure
- Most importantly, plan ahead

Through some very simple planning, television and computers can effectively be tamed to maximize your children's learning potential. So do not worry, to be an effective parent in taming the media tide at this age requires just a few simple steps. But remember, like anything else, it is easier to stem the media tide later if your children have some understanding of balance earlier, so the steps you take with them at this age will more than likely pay off in later years as well.

CHAPTER 3 CHEAT SHEET

TELEVISION

DAILY DOSAGE	There is no excuse to be someone interested enough to buy this book and *not* be below the average: fewer than two hours, preferably one or less.
KEY ADVANTAGE	Educational television.
REMEDY	Become an expert on your children's programming; show only educational television; interact with your child watching television to maximize learning.

COMPUTERS

KEY CONCERN	Many, though currently with little research to support the large amounts of criticism.
KEY ADVANTAGE	Initially requires parental interaction; most preschool software is educational.

ADVERTISING

KEY CONCERN	Preschoolers are capable of watching ads, but not capable of understanding what their purpose is, and certainly not capable of critically interacting with advertising.
REMEDY	Use your DVR and other recording devices and "on-demand" services; interact and skip ads for them.

The Early Elementary Years

AS ONE MIGHT EXPECT, this chapter covers what is by far the most frequently researched and discussed topic of all concerning children and the mass media: the effect of television violence. But other media consumption becomes an even greater concern for parents as their children reach their early elementary years. Have you heard of MySpace? Yes, you might say, but my seven-year-old is years away from having anything to do with such a site. Perhaps that is the case with MySpace, but what is all this about your daughter interacting with all her friends on Club Penguin? Have you even heard of Club Penguin?

But that is not all. These are the years when parents need to start thinking about television filtering (if you haven't already), Internet filtering, online bullying, and video game ratings, to name a few. But the news is not all bad, indeed, far from it. Media can still teach much, and parents need not worry about being "superparents" in order to successfully protect their kids from electronic media. It just takes some knowledge and the incorporation of a few rules and regulations.

Television

I recently asked a friend to name whatever came to mind first when I asked him for a memory from his elementary school TV viewing years. His answer was surprisingly quick: Bugs Bunny.

I have to admit, it was a good answer! Who can forget Bugs and Daffy, Scooby-Doo, and Tom and Jerry (to name a few)? But wait a second . . . all these memories . . . they all involve violence to some degree. Some would argue a lot of violence. And of course, I only mentioned three cartoons of the hundreds of cartoon-based programs for children produced over the last fifty years. Today's cartoons are far more violent, as are many other "live-action" programs.

Television as the Village Storyteller

Hillary Clinton famously said, "It takes a village to raise a child." She was undoubtedly correct. Unfortunately, as many media critics have pointed out, we live in two villages: the one we sleep, eat, and breathe in, and the one we watch, and escape to. In other words, the first village consists of the physical village of our everyday lives. The second village is the village, or indeed, world of television and other mass media.

Think about it for a second. What is it like to, say, be in court? For most of us, we have broken no laws, and perhaps with even a little bit of luck, we have never been called to jury duty! But we all know what court is like, yes? We have, after all, seen it on television a million times.

And what about what it is like to be a teenager? How do we learn about that? If you have an older sibling, they certainly provide a window into that world. And kids all get to see how the big kids act in school. But really, as an older elementary school student, how do we come to know how we should act when we get to middle school? Meet our first boyfriend or girlfriend? Interact with peers? Both villages provide answers. But the important point is, the answers to these questions are more accessible, if not greatly so, on television, though they might not actually be accurate.

Television is the village storyteller. Whether we accept what it has to tell us or not, television does tell us. It offers us a village whether we choose to accept it or not.

We might be smart enough, you say, to reject this reality for "real" reality. There are, however, two problems with that thought. First, much of what television presents us is not "in-your-face." Of course, we see the lead characters for who they are: actors and actresses who may be simple to reject as fictional. But few people consider the accuracy of the background. Consider the crime lab in the popular show, *CSI*. Slick halogen (even nightclub-like) lighting, glass walls, state-of-the-art equipment. Have you ever seen the inside of a real crime lab? Few have. The reality is that many crime labs are cash-strapped, plan-looking basic environments with much more old equipment than new. What is your mind's-eye image of a crime lab? Most certainly, it closely mirrors the *CSI* lab. And of course it does! You have had nothing to counter that image from your real-world experience, and we rarely fight against the background images of television, no matter how much we might bridge the gap between how the characters act on television and what people are like in real-life.

But the more important problem is that we are not talking about you and me in this book . . . we are talking about children. Children are far less equipped to reject what television presents to them. Forget about the background; in most cases, the foreground, the characters and their actions, are rarely, if ever challenged. They are as much a reality as the living room the television sits in.

So it is important to remember that television is not just entertainment, it is reality (because we treat it that way). And with today's proliferation of reality-based shows, there is even less likelihood that we, or our children, challenge how well that reality mirrors the real world.

To sum up this point I have to return to Hillary Clinton's statement. Her statement was meant to underscore that parents cannot do it alone. We do not have all the time in the world to teach our children all the lessons they will learn, to provide them all the support they will need, and teach them all there is to teach. And in Mrs. Clinton's world, that village also comprises our teachers, camp counselors, and neighbors. But we cannot forget that as much as these people interact with our children, so too does television. It tells our children stories. It imbues them with values (good or bad). It teaches them, whether they realize it or not. This can work for the parent or against the parent. For this reason, more than any, parents need to be mindful of what their children watch, especially during the elementary school years. This chapter provides the guidelines and lessons learned to help parents use media wisely, to guide children to get the right values and the right lessons to be gained from television.

Television Violence: What Is It and How Much Is There?

The positive effects of television found in the prior chapter, including learning potential, altruism, prosocial behavior, and even facilitation of imaginative play, hold true throughout the elementary school years. Indeed, as Mares and Woodard put it, the potential impact of television (remember, it matters what type of television, as it must be educational, correctly paced, and appropriate for your child) on prosocial behavior "should serve as something of an antidote to those who consider television to be nothing but detrimental."

Nevertheless, television does have a dark side, and whereas we found in the prior chapter the potential for moderate negative impact on attention, sleep patterns, and obesity, in the present chapter we will review what is considered perhaps the most dangerous effect of television, and that is the impact of its violent content.

You might say, but my elementary school child does not watch violence on television; that comes later, when they are in middle school and high school. But of course, as we remember our own childhood, we come back again to *Bugs Bunny*. And again, Warner Brothers cartoons are just the tip of the iceberg: There is far more violent television out there targeting your third grade child.

How Much Violence Do They See?

So how much violence do children watch? Basic exposure to televised violence is probably far more widespread than one might think. And remember most of the data are based on parental self-reports, which are almost certainly under-reporting the truth. After all, as a typical concerned parent, you would likely be embarrassed to admit that your one-year-old is watching violent television. Research has continually found that a certain percentage of people who are interviewed about behaviors they might be embarrassed about will lie about those behaviors so that they are seen as more virtuous than they really are.

That television is violent is unquestioned. From 1994 to 1997, the largest analysis of television content ever was conducted by the National Cable Television Association. It found that two out of every three programs contained a "violent act." Overall, television was found to contain six violent acts every hour. But most interestingly, this study found children's television to be more violent than adult programming. In fact, just under three out of every four children's programs contained violence. In sum, these researchers found the average child will see about three thousand violent acts every year!

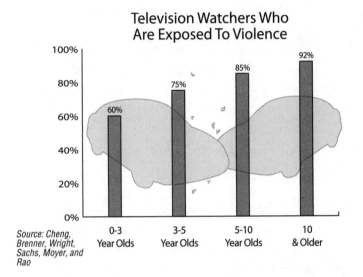

Television Watchers Who Are Exposed To Violence

Source: Cheng, Brenner, Wright, Sachs, Moyer, and Rao

0-3 Year Olds: 60%
3-5 Year Olds: 75%
5-10 Year Olds: 85%
10 & Older: 92%

A common criticism of these types of studies, however, is that they do not discern between types of violent acts. Surely, having the Road Runner lure Wile E. Coyote to fall of a 1,000 foot cliff is less harmful to a child that a child watching the common gun violence of a typical adult cops-and-robbers show.

Indeed, there are many, many kinds of violence, and many differences that make one violent act qualitatively different than another. Some differences noted in the past include:

1. Is it intentional? If violence occurs from an accidental act, does it have the same negative effect as intentional violence?

2. Is there lasting harm? One of the criticisms of people who do not differentiate one violent act from another is that

in a lot of cartoon violence, a character might become the victim of violence, only to be fine two seconds later. For example, in a typical *Bugs Bunny* or *Tom and Jerry* cartoon, a character might get run over by a street paver and get flattened to the width of a piece of paper. But two seconds later, he acts like a bike pump and blows himself back up into three dimensions. Is this as violent as other, more realistic television violence?

3. And what about humorous violence? Are the *Three Stooges* and similiar shows as bad as the realistic violence of other programming?

Unfortunately, studies that have separated out realistic violence from "fantasy violence" (violence that is clearly not realistic) have, nevertheless, found the same effects for both types of violence, though at a lower level for people exposed to fantasy violence and not realistic violence.

Regardless of these differences—differences that make violence on children's programming less shocking and concerning than violence on adult shows—there is another difference between many common kids and adult programming. Programs for kids are disproportionately filled with what is called "sinister combat violence." Simply put, many of these shows are designed around violence. They are shows where fighting is *the* way to solve problems and the better the fighter, the more esteemed the character.

So what are the effects of television violence? As mentioned in an earlier chapter, study of this phenomenon started with the famous Bobo doll experiments by Albert Bandura and colleagues. Again, in these experiments, children who were exposed to a TV clip of someone hitting a life size doll were more likely to imitate such behavior, compared to children who did not see the clip. Importantly, children imitated the behavior even more if the actor in the clip was rewarded for his behavior. So, from this basic set of experiments, scholars believe there to be one very basic effect of violent television, and that is, simply put, that violence begets violence.

Violence Is Normal

Unfortunately, the finding that television violence can lead to real life violence has been shown time after time. And importantly, this link does not just occur in experiments that use made-up videos of adults hitting life-sized dolls. For example, one experiment by Boyatzis, Matillo and Nesbitt compared kids who did not watch TV to a group of children who watched a full episode of *Mighty Morphin Power Rangers*. The kids who watched the *Power Rangers* were found to display seven times the violence (acts such as hitting, shoving, or verbally assaulting another child) than kids who did not watch the show.

In yet another study, Buchanan asked children in the third through fifth grades to identify classmates who have in the past been mean to others through bullying, physical incidents, or verbal aggression. In later surveys of mean as well as other less aggressive or nonaggressive children, children considered "mean" were found to have watched significantly more violent television. The question this study should pose to all parents is, do you want your kid to be a "mean kid" in part because you did not limit their exposure to violent television?

And if that question does not create enough evidence about the link between violent television and actual violence, yet another study by Huesmann that spanned over twenty years found that boys who watched violent television at age eight were found to be more likely to commit crimes as an adult. The vast majority of eight year olds that watch violent television turn out just fine. But at the same time, is this really something about which you want to take a chance?

Researchers have looked at other potential effects of television violence. And they have gotten awfully creative to find such effects. One of the more creative experiments (though not the first to try this approach) requires a full explanation because of the sheer inventiveness of its design (indeed, I have used this one for years in my own research methods class, if anything, just to show that even research scientists can have active imaginations). In the experiment conducted by Molitor and others, children were split into two groups. The first group watched a condensed version of violent scenes from the *The Karate Kid*. The second group watched clips from Olympic competitions (why? To show something as similar as possible to the formal fight scenes in *The Karate Kid*, without the violence).

The experimental scene is this: In a school, a room is set up with toys and a television video camera on a tripod, with wires that trail into a second room. The second room contains a television, in which the wires from the first room are attached. The children are put through the experiment one at a time. Of course, the children have no idea they are part of an experiment. What they are told, as they walk from one room to another with an adult who is acting on behalf of the experiment, is that someone normally uses the video camera to watch children to make sure they behave. Once the child and the adult get into the second room, the television shows children walking into the first room. They start to play with the toys in the room.

Of course, it's all made up: What the adult and child are actually seeing is a videotape. But that adult lies to the child, basically saying, "See, this TV shows us what is going on in the other room." Suddenly, the adult is called to the main office.

The adult asks the child to stay in the room and watch the other children on the television, and that if anything happens they should seek the assistance of an adult. After the adult leaves, the children on the monitor begin arguing over toys. Quickly, the argument becomes a tussle, with hair pulling and shoving, and eventually, the children bump the camera, which falls over sideways and eventually turns to static.

What does this experiment prove? Was there any difference between the child who watched the violent fight scenes from the *The Karate Kid* and the one who watched the exciting but nonviolent clips from the Olympics? You bet: The children who watched the *The Karate Kid* took 37 seconds to decide to get help from the onset of witnessing the children "in the other room" argue and fight. But the children who watched the Olympics took only 21 seconds to do the same.

In short, what this experiment demonstrates is that television violence desensitizes one to "real life" violence. We are, in short, more tolerant of violence, less concerned when we witness it. Similar experiments have also given children hypothetical "conflict situations" to discuss after the experiment, with the goal in mind of finding out how the children might react differently to them. Those children who watch violent television were much more likely to offer an aggressive solution to these situations than the children who watched nonviolent television.

Violence Is Just Everyday Life

Yet another important impact of violent television is based on the television having become our village storyteller. We have two "realities" telling us about reality: Actual, real-life experience, and our televised experience. Because we tend to not "get around" in real-life nearly as much as we do in television, we tend to take what we see in television, and not in real life, as reflective of real life. Again, most of us have never been in a crime lab, so we tend to think they look just like the one on the popular television series, *CSI*.

One of the major problems with this is that people (luckily!) tend to never witness violent crimes in-person. But we see an awful lot of them on the television. What this leads to is what researchers call the "mean-world syndrome." That is, we tend to think the real world is as violent as the televised world. Fortunately, the real world is far, far less violent than the television world. But in one sense, what does that matter if we treat the real world as *if* it is as violent as its fictitious televised portrayals?

So in short, the more television we watch, the more violence we see, and the more we think the real world is filled with violence. This can lead to us being more antisocial, more afraid of the outside world, and more prone to aggression ourselves. These are not attitudes we strive to instill in our children.

Certainly I could spend scores of additional pages discussing study after study regarding television and violence. There have, after all, been over 1,000 studies conducted on the subject. But the point, I think, has been made. Science shows that television violence has many effects on people, and none of them are good. And the general public largely understands this fact. Seventy-five percent of Americans believe that televised violence contributes to real world crime and aggression. By the age of eighteen, it is estimated that a person will have witnessed over 200,000 violent acts of murder, rape and other physical crimes. And this does not even include the majority of fantasy violence or non-physical acts of aggression. Add those to the mix and the average eighteen-year-old just might witness a half a million such acts.

"Combating" Violence

All this violence does not transform the average child into a killer. No one has really argued that that is the case. Certainly, for someone to become a criminal, much, much else must have happened in that person's life than just watching *Rambo* on television. But as parents, our concern is not so much whether our kids will become killers thanks to television. There are other more likely outcomes from violent television that are, while not as terrible, still quite disconcerting for the concerned parent. Do I want my kid to fear the real world? Do I want my kid to sit around and watch another kid get hurt and not go for help? And finally, do I want my child to be the aggressive one, perhaps even a bully to her peers? Of course not. Again it is important to note that violent television alone usually will not trigger such behavior in a child. But a review of the vast volume of research out there suggests that watching violence on television will increase the chance your child behaves aggressively by at least ten percent. That is a level at which most parents should be concerned, for none of us want our kid to be the bad apple. So what do we do? Here are a few options:

1. *Prohibit your child from watching television.* This is yet again the answer of many media critics. It's not realistic. Few parents could ever achieve this. And then, it's something they could only achieve in their own home. So forget about this one, and let's move on!

2. *Prohibit your child from watching* violent *television.* Boy, does that sound good! Think you can do it? Again, in the words of a famously violent television character, "fugget-a-bout it." The problem is, violence pervades all programming. Yes, there are children's programs that are nonviolent. But these tend to be targeting preschoolers or very early

elementary school children. Yes, there are nonviolent programs out there for elementary school and older children, for example, *Bill Nye the Science Guy*. But they are in the minority. Even seemingly harmless shows, such as *Scooby-Doo* and *The Flintstones* contain some level of violence. Most slapstick shows, such as *Bugs Bunny* and *Tom and Jerry*, contain violent acts. And let's not even talk about superhero shows: They are premised upon violent behavior. Certainly, parents should do what they can to minimize exposure to shows that are clearly inappropriate for their child. As we learned in the previous chapter, it is important to prohibit your children from watching adult programming during their elementary school years. So even though you will never be perfect in achieving this, it is still important to do what you can to limit the amount of violent television your child watches.

3. *Do you know what your child is watching?* It should go without saying that if your child is watching a show that you have never seen before, you should stop what you are doing and watch ten minutes with her. If you cannot find the time, and have a DVR, hit the record button and watch it later that evening. You do not have to watch every show your child watches, all the time. But doing so allows you to assess the level of violence on the show, as well as other aspects of violent content described below. If you cannot watch the show the first time your child watches it, that's okay. One viewing of an inappropriate show is not going to permanently scar your child for life. But do try to watch a bit of that show fairly quickly after your child has.

4. *When aggression or violence happens, how does it happen?* If one cannot completely avoid violence on television, one can at least understand that some violence is not as negative as others. First, violence that happens to clearly bad people

as punishment for bad actions, in the case of some super-hero violence, has been shown to have a less harmful effect on children. If at all possible, characters who act violently should either get punished for it, or be punishing someone who acted violently without cause in the first place.

5. *Talk to your children about violence.* Make sure your children understand that while fantasy violence may be to some degree entertaining, violence or aggression in the real world is not acceptable and will be punished. When a violent act occurs on television without punishment, explain to your child that such actions are unacceptable. Just as we discussed in the prior chapter, it is vitally important to contextualize television for your children. Explain to them why things are happening, what kind of behavior is unrealistic, and what behavior would not be tolerated in the real world.

6. *Understand television ratings and use your V-Chip.* The good news for parents is that a lot of the work with regard to violence on television has already been done for them, thanks to television ratings and the V-chip. The bad news is, too few parents are even aware of such things, and fewer still are using them. Yet understanding television ratings takes all of about two minutes, and setting up the V-chip about the same amount of time.

The Importance of the V-Chip

Actually, the V-chip is not even a chip. And it is easy to use. The V-chip is nothing more than the same programming logic and circuitry that controls closed captioning and other television controls. The circuitry reads information that is sent along with the programming signal to tell the television or cable box the rating of each show. The user can then set up that television or cable box to only allow shows of a certain threshold rating, meaning that programs for that age group or younger can pass through.

So understanding and controlling a V-Chip is akin to having a television "nanny," that monitors the ratings of each show. Thus, using the V-chip necessitates understanding television ratings.

Most parents do not seem to understand these things, so learning the ratings system is the first necessary step. True, about two-thirds of parents say they know of the V-Chip, and even more know of television ratings. But as we have learned, parents often notoriously do not tell the truth in surveys, but rather tell interviewers what they think they want to hear. True enough, when tested about what each rating means, half of all parents give the wrong response. (Even more concerning about this is that quite a few of these questions were two-choice questions, so even if parents were making wild guesses they would still, on average, be right half the time.)

There is one very simple explanation for why parents don't really know what the television ratings mean: No one has ever explained them. Additionally, they are more complicated than the simplicity of, say, movie ratings. But that is no excuse. After all, there are only six of them.

These ratings are selected for each show by the television industry. The makers of original programming rate their programs and channels that show syndicated shows (that is, reruns of older running shows) are responsible for rating the shows they air.

As you can see, the ratings themselves are not that difficult to understand, though they are certainly more complicated than the movie ratings we are all used to. Yet as I have shown, it is likely that over half of all parents do not fully understand them. But while we can all blame ourselves for not going out there and educating ourselves about these definitions, the

Television Ratings Explained

Below are the official explanations of the ratings, according to the TV Parental Guidelines board:

 All Children: Designed to be appropriate for all children. Whether animated or live-action, the themes and elements in this program are specifically designed for a very young audience, including children from ages 2—6. This program is not expected to frighten younger children.

 Directed to Older Children: For children age 7 and above. It may be more appropriate for children who have acquired the developmental skills needed to distinguish between make-believe and reality. Themes and elements in this program may include mild fantasy violence or comedic violence, or may frighten children under the age of seven. Therefore, parents may wish to consider the suitability of this program for their very young children.

 Directed to Older Children—Fantasy Violence: For those programs where fantasy violence may be more intense or more combative than other programs in this category, such programs will be designated TV-Y7-FV.

 General Audience: Most parents would find this program suitable for all ages. Although this rating *does not signify a program designed specifically for children*, most parents may let younger children watch this program unattended. It contains little or no violence, no strong language and little or no sexual dialogue or situations.

(continued)

 Parental Guidance Suggested: This program contains material that parents may find unsuitable for younger children. Many parents may want to watch it with their younger children. The theme itself may call for parental guidance and/or the program contains one or more of the following: moderate violence (V), some sexual situations (S), infrequent coarse language (L), or some suggestive dialogue (D).

 Parents Strongly Cautioned: This program contains some material that many parents would find unsuitable for children under 14 years of age. Parents are strongly urged to exercise greater care in monitoring this program and are cautioned against letting children under the age of 14 watch unattended. This program contains one or more of the following: intense violence (V), intense sexual situations (S), strong coarse language (L), or intensely suggestive dialogue (D).

 Mature Audience Only: This program is specifically designed to be viewed by adults and therefore may be unsuitable for children under 17. This program contains one or more of the following: graphic violence (V), explicit sexual activity (S), or crude indecent language (L).

Source: www.fcc.gov *and TV Parental Guidelines Monitoring Board*

information about these ratings is not entirely easy to access if one does not search for it via the Internet (think of, for example, the many adults who still do not frequently browse the Internet).

Now that you understand the ratings, you are halfway there! The second part is knowing how to apply them. And this is exactly what the V-chip is for: To tell your television what it is allowed to show and what it is prohibited to show. Unfortunately, I cannot walk you through the process of activating your V-chip, since every television or cable box has a different method of turning the V-chip filter on. Regardless, every television set manufactured after the year 2000 is capable of screening for material. For most digital cable boxes, there should be an option once the menu button is selected to go to parental controls. Most television sets have a menu button on their remote.

The typical parental control menu will allow you to do two things. First, you may select a level of filtering. This system is fairly straightforward, allowing any program that has a more mature rating to automatically be blocked if you choose to filter at a lower level. For example, selecting TV-Y7 will filter not only shows at TV-Y7 but also programs at every other higher level up to TV-MA. The second thing the menu is going to do is to ask for a passcode. This is so that your children are not readily able to turn off your filtering. Make sure if your child was born on 10/10/02 that you do not use 101002 as your passcode!

One big problem with the V-chip is that these menu programs often do not discriminate. So when you and your spouse curl up and watch the latest made-for-TV thriller, you are probably going to find that you are blocked as well! But with a little experience, it quickly becomes second nature to enter in your code when needed.

The beauty of the ratings system, coupled with the V–chip, is that as a parent, you only need to set it up once (well okay, every few years you will want to change what ratings are allowed to be seen). So why don't more parents use the chip? Most parents do not use the chip because they actually

Filters You Should Be Using by Age . . .

Certainly, you are the judge of what you want to allow your child to watch. But here are typical guidelines you can follow:

UNDER AGE 3
Nothing . . . they should not be watching anything you do not know about anyway!

AGE 3 TO 6
TV-Y7. This will block any shows meant for children ages seven and older. However, older children may be permitted to watch some of these. It is a judgment call as to when your child can handle a higher rating. Additionally, this decision is not easy because there is ambiguity between a TV-Y7 program and the next level, TV-G, as TV-G is described as a rating indicating that it is okay for "younger children" to watch.

AGE 7 TO 10
TV-G to TV-PG. Again, there are no absolute rules as to whether to allow your child to view shows only up to TV-G or to allow PG as well. My recommendation is to stay with G until double digits (ages ten and older).

AGE 11 TO 13
TV-PG. This general rating is a good limit for preteens.

AGE 14 TO 18
TV-14. The earlier years of this age group should be limited to TV-14. Later years might be suitable for TV-MA as well. After all, you are now dealing with young adults who are able (at least in many cases), and certainly willing (better put, demanding) to choose their own path.

do not understand the ratings. Others just do not realize the chip exists. But in today's world of digital cable and digital televisions, it is easier than ever to utilize it. My cable box, in fact, comes with the ability to limit viewing by television rating as well as movie ratings. Additionally you can program it to not show adult channels on the preview guides or as previews in its "On Demand" video feature. In about three minutes of time one can set up the television to protect your kids for years to come. Of all the advice presented in this book, nothing could be simpler.

Continuing to Learn from Television

Just as with preschoolers, there is quite a bit that early elementary school children can learn from television. Research consistently shows a number of effects similar to those already covered in the prior chapter. Because of its visual element and potential for interactivity, television has the capability of "making it stick" more effectively than reading. That is, television more frequently wins out over reading for memory retention. Not that I am suggesting you pull that book away from your child and plant him in front of the television! The research on the link between both high reading ability and a high number of hours dedicated to reading and scholastic and professional achievement is consistently strong.

Television can, however, teach vocabulary, words, and letters. As your children get older, they gain more and more of an ability to learn things such as words and letters from television. A wealth of programs promote reading and vocabulary skills for preschool and early elementary children. So seek out such shows and make sure the television your children do watch includes such programming.

You have also learned that preschoolers can gain a positive impact of prosocial behavior from television. But how much prosocial behavior is on TV? How does that compare to antisocial behavior? It turns out, at least in the earlier programming of the 1970s, that there are equal amounts of both. A more recent study, however, found that only four percent of children's shows that were violent had an anti-violence message as well. Yet another study found that the amount of prosocial content in children's television grew 25 percent. Importantly, it is not just how much violence there is on television, it is whether that violence has some justifiable punishment or some other anti-violence message. This way, kids are taught about prosocial behaviors by watching good examples as well as bad examples that are immediately corrected.

Learning to Read . . . from Television?

Modern televisions are all able to receive closed-captioned information to display on the screen. In one interesting study by Linebarger, researchers tested whether having these captions on during a typical children's television program improved word recognition. Captions also appeared to "focus" children, allowing them to recall specific elements of the show that were more related to central, thematic, and character elements as compared to less central elements (in the example provided by the authors, an element that was less central was that a "bunny character had red ears").

Parents can turn on the closed captioning feature of their televisions. Alternatively, they can seek out shows that feature a significant amount of captioning. For example, *Read Between the Lions* and *Super WHY* are shows that specifically use captioning that allows viewers to read the book as the story unfolds; it also has elements where captioning is used to teach letters and spelling.

How Much is Too Much?

When it comes to general exposure to television there are, of course, the usual warnings, the same you learned in the previous chapter. First, do not overload your children with television. Four hours a day is too much. Indeed, some studies suggest that heavy television watching from elementary school through middle school is linked to lower achievement scores in school, though other, somewhat more rigorous studies tend to find no relationship between heavy viewing and academic achievement

It might be the case, though, that the lack of effect is because of something called "mainstreaming." What this means, simply put, is that television takes children who are otherwise diverse and makes them similar to one another, and specifically, heavy television viewing tends to increase the aptitude of children in families in low income classes, while lowering the achievement scores of children growing up in high income families. Researchers are not entirely certain why this is the case, though some think that children in high income environments tend to spend free time doing educational activities more often than children in lower income families. Thus, all that time spent in front of the television takes away from educational activities of high income children, while, on average, increasing educational activities (via educational programming and other learning from television) for low income families. Whatever your household income, there is little excuse for more television. Your best strategy is to allow television in moderation, focusing on the most educational programming available.

Also, programming matters. I am not just talking about protecting your child from violent television. I am talking about knowing what your child watches from program to program and maximizing exposure to educational television and minimizing noneducational programming. Co-viewing also helps tremendously. But even without co-viewing, by this age, most children are much better able to learn from television regardless of your interaction. So let them watch, but not too much, and especially the right kind.

When and How to Introduce the News to Children

One aspect of television that is sometimes perplexing for parents is the news. The news exposes people to the larger

Live Shows = Good; Cartoons = Bad?

The "common" thinking about television programs is that "real character" shows (either one hundred percent live or mostly live) like *Mister Rogers' Neighborhood*, *Sesame Street*, and *The Wiggles* are inherently better than cartoons. This thinking is based primarily on the fact that most experiments have compared cartoons to real-character shows and found the real-character shows to be superior on a number of levels. But it is important to note that in the majority of these studies it was not something inherent in the cartoons that made them less desirable. Rather, it just so happened the cartoon shows selected in these experiments served as the "bad" condition for other reasons. For example if a researcher wanted to explore violent children's television to nonviolent television, he or she was most likely to compare one of the "usual" nonviolent shows as *Mister Rogers* and the like, and the violent show as a typical cartoon like *Batman* or *Teenage Mutant Ninja Turtles*.

But cartoons are not in-and-of-themselves inherently bad. Indeed, some cartoons clearly have significantly high educational value. *WordGirl*, for example, is a "superheroine" show, but one where the main character is focused on learning vocabulary. Other cartoons are similarly educational, and in some respects, they have the added advantage of, being animated, which some think are more appealing to children than live-character shows.

world. It can underscore the issues a civilized and democratic society faces. But on the other hand, news, especially local news, can often contain much violence, some of it graphic, and all of it very, very real. Studies have clearly shown that realistic violence is far scarier and disturbing than fictional violence. I clearly remember being thirteen and visiting a museum in Israel where an exhibit showed footage from the Six Day War. Despite being a "war buff," what caught my eye was seeing Israeli soldiers drop to the ground in ways that were clearly not natural. They were in fact, being shot. And though the footage was grainy and from a far distance, the effect it had on me was unlike any fictionalized violence I had seen in the movies or TV. These people were actually *dying*.

Certainly, television news rarely shows such graphic violence. Typically what we see is the aftermath. But it is real, and let's face it, that makes a substantial difference. So does the news teach good civics and worldly concern for others, or does is scare our children into thinking we live in a mean, ultraviolent world? (And the things to be scared at from the news don't end with the local feed on the latest murder in the city. There is plenty else to worry about, including hurricanes, terrorists, and even toy recalls.)

Are young children watching the evening news? According to Kaiser data, Nearly two thirds of eleven to sixteen year olds watch the news on a typical weeknight. Among elementary school children, the percentage is lower at about forty percent. Nevertheless, about two-thirds of elementary school children watch the news at least "sometimes" if not everyday.

Similarly, around sixty-six percent of older children (eight to twelve year olds) say the news sometimes scares or upsets them. A study of the space shuttle *Challenger* explosion found elementary school children emotionally upset for over a week after the event. Another example is war footage. Studies by Smith and Wilson as well as other researchers have found that nearly half of parents of children in grades one through eleven claimed their children had been upset of frightened by the news coverage of the first Persian Gulf War.

There is a point at which children start to become less scared of fantasy dangers (monsters, etc.) and more concerned with realistic dangers. This shift comes to most children some-time in the middle of their elementary school years. Similarly, as children improve their cognitive faculties, verbal commu-nication takes on greater significance. It has been found that younger children need the visual elements of television news to show dangerous things in order for them to get fright-ened, older children less so. Interestingly, younger elementary school children are more likely to be scared by disaster stories, as compared to older elementary school children, who more frequently are scared by crime stories.

Of course, not only have studies found the news to be scary to children, news has been shown to be just as chilling to us adults. So using "scare potential" as a yardstick for when to start exposing children to the news is not an effective mea-sure. Thus we need something else by which to make a judg-ment call on this. The best place to start is to figure out when children actually understand that the news is informational. About halfway though elementary school, most children are able to distinguish a picture of a news anchor from a picture of an actor. Children around this age are also able to define the goal of the news in contrast to other programming. And finally, older children are much better able to discuss the news appropriately with parents, meaning they understand it enough, and process enough of it, to retain the information presented to them and convey that information to others. As might be expected, older elementary school children are much better able to recall news stories than younger elementary school students.

The research on the introduction of news to children provides clear suggestions as to how to do it effectively. Here are some tips:

1. *Explain What the News Is.* It is important to note that to most children the news is one of the first types of unintended watching of television they receive. Thus many children will watch the news without first understanding what it is or why mommy and daddy watch it. So, beat them to the chase and explain to them that the news is important because humans live in communities.

2. *Inoculate Your Child from News Violence.* Explain to your child early that the news sometimes talks about bad things that happen in the world. Explain to them that the world is full of good people doing good deeds, but that the news tends to talk about the bad people and bad deeds out there so that we can understand how we need to improve as a society. Explain to them that the crime they might see will probably never happen in their home (they will figure out for themselves that is not entirely the case anyway!).

3. *Bring Out a Map.* Another fun activity to do with children when they watch news is to show them on a map where things are happening. This can give them a greater interest in the larger world as well as increase interest in the news itself.

4. *Watch the News Interactively.* Because the news tends to be one of the first "adult" programs children watch, it is important to watch it with them interactively because there will be much, much more to explain to them than with a typical children's program. Again, train them to

watch the news in a way that does not scare them and which provides them with a greater appreciation of the outside world.

Suggestions for Elementary School Children

In the previous chapters we learned when to introduce television, what to look out for, and how to have your children watch (interactively and not in their own rooms). In this chapter we learned about television's most harmful effect, that of violence and aggression. We learned about the benefits of television on prosocial behavior and discovered how to introduce the news. In short, the lesson of this chapter is exposure. The concern is not just quantity but rather quality. The great news is, you have the power to control quality to a large extent with just five minutes of your time, by learning to use and utilizing the V-chip and subsequent television ratings. I cannot underscore enough how easy yet powerful the chip can be in limiting bad television. Additionally, though, we learned that there is programming out there that may be appropriate for your child even though its rating is higher than the general one you use on your chip, or is otherwise an adult program, as is the case generally with the news. As with prior chapters of this book, the most important element to reduce the harmful impact of more adult shows is intermediation, that is, watching some programming with your child and contextualizing what you see. As a quick review, here are some of the mediation strategies that will have the most positive impact on your child:

1. *Correcting Bad Behavior:* Make sure you make it clear to your children that such behavior would never be tolerated in your home.

2. *Readjusting the Frequency of Bad Behavior and News:* Tell your children that such things rarely happen in real life because in real life people tend to be good, have families that care about them, and behave accordingly.

3. *When They Do Get Scared, Treat Them Like Children:* Don't brush these instances off with a quick "act like an adult" routine. The strategies mentioned in the prior chapter still apply to elementary school children. Love them, hug them, and otherwise give them interactions that allow the stress hormones to dissipate from their young bodies and minds.

Oh yes, and remember that V-chip!

Computers and the Internet

Well, the time has come. Your child is only seven years old, and she wants to "chat" on the Internet! What is this world coming to?

Well, in truth, it is not coming to anything. It has just changed out from under you and now you are the one that is struggling to be relevant and with it. The problem is, kids don't quite have that problem. You had to learn to understand the Internet. And in truth, the numbers show, most of us really don't. But for those who grow up immersed in a technology, such technology is second nature. While we are trying to understand how to work our iPhones, our kids are taking them apart to understand how they work!

Children's Internet knowledge and abilities grow fast. In the words of one five-year-old child studied by author ZhenYan, the Internet "has two computers on it ... It has toys and games. It wouldn't hurt you." This same author found that it does not take long for this view to change, both in the number of computers that are linked as well as whether it can hurt you.

There is not much information on early elementary school students and their Internet use. But according to data from a few years ago on four through six-years-olds, it becomes quite clear that at least half of seven through nine-year-olds are using the Internet.

As we have seen in the previous chapter, the majority of four through six-year-olds can use a mouse and have spent time on a computer by themselves. But what about the Internet specifically? Nearly one-third of four through six-year-olds have gone to a children's website *on their own*. A smaller percentage has used e-mail with the help of an adult.

U.S. Census data shows a tremendous jump in Internet use amongst seven to nine-year-olds. Around fifteen percent of this age group had accessed the Internet in 1997. Four years later that figure had reached an astonishing forty-five percent. Today, largely thanks to Internet access in schools, that number is thought to be as high as seventy-five percent.

Research on older children by the U.S. Department of Education (nine years through nineteen) shows what you probably already know: Children are Internet savvy. They use it, and with a dexterity that far surpasses that of most adults. This places adults at a disadvantage, since they increasingly know less about the Internet and show less proficiency at using it and other online media like e-mail, instant messaging, and chat rooms. Many parents do not limit their children's Internet use simply because they do not know how, or are intimidated by the technology into even trying.

Of course, that is where this book comes in. Adding Internet filters is easy. And tracking what your children see on the Internet is just as easy. So just like using the V-chip, here is an example where an ounce of prevention is worth a pound of cure. Do a few small things to set up your computer for use by children and you are well on your way to protecting your child from the dangers of the Internet.

Certainly, setting up a typical "cyber nanny" on your computer is not all you need to do. We will leave those topics—online predators, bullying, identity security, pornography, and general Internet addiction—for later chapters. The focus at this stage should be on prevention.

What Does an Eight Year Old Do Online Anyway?

First, it might be good to discuss what children in their early elementary years do online. According to the National Center for Educational Statistics, as well as data by Kaiser, about half of children this age who go online use e-mail with the assistance of an adult. Pretty much all children of this age group use the computer and to some extent the Internet to play games. One question some parents have is whether kids of this age can actually type. In fact, generally, preschoolers can only recognize letters on the keyboard and spell their own names and perhaps a few other limited words. The more they play games on the computer, the more they gain a familiarity with the keyboard.

Early elementary school children, on the other hand, can "hunt and peck" on the keyboard, and by the time they become preteens, will likely have some familiarity with where the most often used letters are. In the preteen years, kids will become more and more proficient by typing schoolwork and through formal typing instruction in the middle or even high school years.

So early elementary school children can, to varying levels, use a keyboard well enough to use the Internet at a cursory level (or better). Unfortunately, there is a lack of formal understanding as to what kids at this age do online; the bulk of the research on children and the Internet begins at around nine years of age and goes upward to eighteen and nineteen-year-olds. So no matter what we do in this chapter, the goal is to have parents "get there first," thereby shielding your kids from anything inappropriate they might wander to by accident or on purpose.

One thing parents should understand is this: Your late elementary school kid already thinks she is better than you are at using the Internet. Indeed, in a comprehensive study of kids in the United Kingdom, seven percent of nine to eleven-year-olds think they are "expert" users; another twenty percent said "advanced" and fifty-five percent said "average." In short, eighty-three percent of these youngsters think they are at least relatively proficient at the Internet. This compares to only two percent of parents who consider themselves expert, another twelve as advanced, and overall, seventy-six percent are at least proficient. Overall, children are better than parents at just about everything they do with a computer.

So, much, much more about what kids do with a computer in the next chapter. But one thing is certain. A strong minority of children ages seven through nine use the Internet in multiple ways, including instant messaging, web browsing, chatting, games, and music. Generally, children's first experience on the Internet is with their parents. Typically children are introduced to a computer sometime between the ages of three and seven. This initial age of introduction, amount of parental support, and total amount of time spent on the computer, will determine how one child's computer skills compare to another. Often the first sites kids go to, via the guidance of a parent, are, unsurprisingly, the website versions of their favorite television shows. The other "first contact" kids might have is through parents bringing them to websites of interest for a particular subject, such as trains or animals. But more typically, it is all about the shows, and luckily many of the website versions of the programs are interactive and fairly educational. They include drawing activities, elementary games such as matching or races, and of course, more information about the show itself (more on the question of whether we are training our kids to be too consumeristic shortly). Some shows have links to other educational sites.

So many children are introduced to the Internet through their parents. Many others are introduced by teachers and school. Regardless, if kids don't get the skills at home they are very likely (if not certain) to get the skills at school. Each grade tends to have its own benchmarks on computer proficiency. If you look at computer curricula around the United States, you will find that your kid is very likely learning the following at school:

- **Kindergarten:** mouse use, two-hand keyboard use, use of special keyboard characters (backspace, etc.), basic icon navigation, basic software navigation, computer painting.
- **First Grade:** save and retrieving documents, basic desktop publishing, open an Internet browser, conduct a computer search, basic sentence typing.
- **Second Grade:** basic spreadsheet use and/or multimedia presentation, Internet bookmarks/favorites, reinforce typing skills.
- **Third Grade:** typing to ten words per minute, advanced file management, access websites with addresses, basic word processing skills.
- **Fourth Grade:** advanced keyboard use (hotkeys and shortcuts), twelve words per minute, use of electronic research sources, e-mail, Internet safety, grammatical editing.

- **Fifth Grade:** scanner and digital camera use, fifteen words per minute, netiquette, database manipulation, advanced Internet searching, advanced word processing.
- **Sixth Grade:** advanced Internet history and use, twenty words per minute, file extensions for graphics, video, etc., understand plagiarism, use of all Microsoft Office programs.
- **Seventh and Eight Grade:** thirty words per minute, advanced use of peripherals, advanced use of Internet resources.

But more than from anywhere else, kids learn from their peers. What they learn, in addition to possible skill-sets already mentioned, is what to do and where to go. When I was in the second grade I distinctly remember learning what other kids were watching on television, and having the desire to watch the same shows. Kids today interact like that too, only now it's not just television but video games, computers and the Internet as well.

However, there are differences between learning what to see on television and where to go on the Internet. Namely, the Internet has many, many more places one can go than a television has channels to change. A parent cannot scroll through the *TV Guide* to see where their kid might go on the Internet. With millions of WebPages, an "Internet Guide" would be impossible. Secondly, the Internet is different than television because on the Internet, kids can tell other kids of places where they can communicate with other kids (and potentially adults).

Indeed, the Internet serves as a location for many avenues of communication. Kids being kids, many of these places amount to "virtual clubs" where you are either in or out. And amazingly, even seven-year-olds might be tuned into such places.

Social Networking for Kids

Are you a member of MySpace or Facebook? If not, you'd be hard pressed to not have at least heard of such places. But what about ClubPenguin? Nicktropolis? At least Webkinz? All three are the basic clubs for early elementary school students. In each, children take on an "avatar," a virtual representation of themselves that others can see online. The choice in ClubPenguin is a penguin of some sort. The choices are much more diverse in the other places mentioned above. In each of these places, kids can create their own chat rooms; they can play games online together and essentially have virtual playdates. Of course, media critics bemoan that virtual playmates are poor replacements for real playdates, and they may have a point. Nevertheless, the point here is that these things are out there, and your kids very well may find them.

Webkinz is a recent phenomenon where kids essentially buy a stuffed animal that comes with a secret code kids can use on the Webkinz website to "adopt" them as pets. They can set up homes for their pets in a virtual world online, and play games to accrue "kinzCash" to buy things for their virtual world and even for their real life stuffed animal. Club-Penguin similarly has games that award cash to buy things for their virtual igloos. And in case you think these sites are not popular, consider that in 2006, the number of unique visitors to the website was over two million.

Most of these sites have extensive safety features, including set dialogue (kids chat by selecting only from possible words they can use), filters, monitors, and the like. These limit in two ways: They prevent unwanted visitors from joining in and they prevent kids from putting out too much personal or offensive information. While these sites may be safe from crime, there is one thing not all sites are safe from: advertising. While some (ClubPenguin) are ad-free, others (Nicktropolis) are not.

While some may consider such online use by young children odd or even disconcerting, most see these sites as harmless, as long as they are used in moderation. They do provide opportunities for learning in general and computer literacy skills in particular. The older generations of us may find online socializing odd, but the one thing they cannot deny is that for newer generations, it is the norm.

Setting Up a Safe Internet Environment

I intend to end this chapter's discussion on the Internet with some tips on what you can do as a parent to utilize the Internet effectively for your children.

In 2005, the Pew Internet and American Life Project found that fifty-four percent of families with children ages 12 through 17 had an Internet filter of some kind in place. (Interestingly, only about twenty-five percent of teenagers think their parents have a filter in place. So either the children are clueless or the parents are fudging their numbers to look good.) Based on some more research, as few as a third of all parents of children ages one through seventeen have Internet filtering. Of course, when surveyed, it becomes clear that these thirty-three percent with filtering in place are those who are most concerned with exposure to sexual material. They also tend to trust their children less regarding what they might be doing on the Internet and, generally speaking, are the most Internet-savvy of all parents.

Considering the threats the Internet poses to children, including online predators, identity theft, and pornography, to name a few, it seems incredible that only a third is filtering

Internet content, and even fewer are monitoring where their children go. There is certainly, for many parents, an intimidation factor in trying to "out-tech" the person considered the family Internet guru: your son or daughter. Yet seventy percent of parents are concerned that their children might give out personal information and would view sexually explicit sites. At the same time, sixty percent of parents think the dangers of the Internet and children are overblown. That is why you should get up to speed now, before your early-elementary school kid does!

Okay, so you are ready to tackle the task, no matter how high or low your computer confidence is. What is the first step? The first step is to find Internet filtering software. There are a few options for this. First, your Internet Service Provider may have software. Such is the case with services like AmericaOnline. Even if you have Internet access via your cable provider, you can usually go to their homepage for subscribers and access software there. If this option seems a little daunting to you, or does not pan out, then just go to the store (either online or in your neighborhood). Pretty much any home office supply or computer store will have software available for purchase, including the popular CyberSitter or CyberPatrol. Some of these programs have a subscription fee, so take a minute to compare programs on one of the store's Internet sites. These programs have setup wizards that explain the options and give you choices. In general, these programs will block unwanted materials (text, pictures, and video). They can also only permit access to materials considered appropriate for kids (each software program makes this judgment differently, though. However, you can usually have some say in what is considered inappropriate). Importantly, you will be able to set different types of restrictions for different members of the family.

Looking Ahead Down the Internet Superhighway

Talking about the early elementary years is a great time to look at how much a threat the Internet might be to your child down the road.

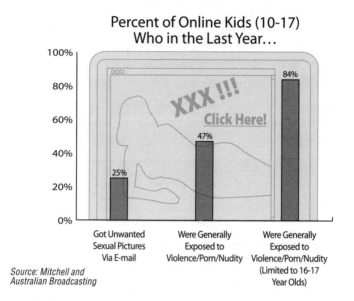

Percent of Online Kids (10-17) Who in the Last Year...

84%	Were Generally Exposed to Violence/Porn/Nudity (Limited to 16-17 Year Olds)
47%	Were Generally Exposed to Violence/Porn/Nudity
25%	Got Unwanted Sexual Pictures Via E-mail

Source: Mitchell and Australian Broadcasting

Three quarters of sex crimes from online contact occur during ages thirteen to fifteen. And nearly half of children "fall for it": In a recent study designed to see if kids would respond to bait online, forty-five percent of ten to seventeen-year-olds were willing to give out their name, address, and other information for a $100 free gift card. So take the time now to protect your kids. Even if you think your child is safe, why not practice doing these things now so that when they are most at risk in their later years, you are an expert at filtering and monitoring?

One concern people might have regarding these programs is whether they filter not just the sites themselves but the listings of inappropriate sites on the usual web search engines like Yahoo and Google. They can, and do so fairly well. They can also block advertising but display the rest of the page.

Finally, you can set these programs up to monitor where your children are going. Not only can you view where they have gone, but in many programs you can set your computer up to take periodic snapshots of the screen so you can actually see what your child has seen.

Periodically, these programs might prompt you via e-mail or via an update upon software setup to get updated. Make sure you do this. Refer to instructions from the help menu of your Internet browser.

Overseeing the Internet: Beyond Filters

There are three major Internet uses that parents can teach their child to use properly, thus teaching and protecting them: one-on-one conversations (e-mail and instant messages), group conversations (chats), and surfing the Internet itself (web browsing).

These tips will provide a very safe household for which to allow your child to "freely" explore the Internet. Establishing these as early as possible will make your child feel less restricted as such practices continue throughout their childhood.

With the growth of sites like ClubPenguin, children are not just going on the Internet but also chatting with others. Chatting is perhaps one of the greatest differences between parents and kids with regard to their online practices, in the sense that children do it a lot, and parents, well, don't. Many, never! So if there is one area at which even tech-savvy parents get a little intimidated, it is with chatting.

The main tip with regard to chatting is to supervise. Again, talk to your child about never giving out any personal information online. And make a rule that they are never allowed to chat unless you are present, at least until you trust them with certain sites.

Most kids will start to use instant messaging and e-mail before their tenth birthday. The dangers of e-mail, like chatting, are that strangers can pretend to be someone else without your child realizing it. Spam can also be quite a problem. If you have had an e-mail account for a long time, you may be used to spam and not even notice it (or if you are like me

What Else Can Parents Do Besides Setting Up Filters? (Early Elementary Tips)

Here are tips to set up a safe environment and keep it that way:

1. Teach your child what to do when he sees something that makes him feel scared or in any way uncomfortable. Coach him to keep whatever "it" is on the screen and come and get mom or dad.
2. Make sure the computer is always in a public space of the house. The best spot is a place that can be seen from both the kitchen and the living room, the two most often used rooms in a house.
3. Start discussing the different types of material you see online, including advertising and links. Explain the Internet to them. In short, give them knowledge about what it is they are using.
4. Make sure your child understands they are, at this age, never allowed to give out ANY personal information, including their name, street name, or anything else, without your permission.
5. Set a rule that if they want to try a game on a site you have never seen that they must show you the game as well. This will limit the chances of playing violent or otherwise inappropriate games.

it drives you crazy!). However, a considerable percentage of spam is adult-oriented. And spammers do not differentiate between children and adults.

Parents should, above all else, share their child's first e-mail account with them. Stronger still, many parents opt to have e-mail access available only to them, meaning that for a child to get e-mail access, he has to ask their parents to type in a password for them. Parents can then review e-mail either with the child or before their child gets access (before is better if you have a spam problem as you can delete the junk before your child sees it). This prevents children from deleting files before parents can see them.

At this "early" age, the dangers of the Internet are not yet apparent, or at least only to a fraction of what they will be in later years. But as a parent, don't you want to protect them before the dangers appear? The Internet offers great opportunity, and great peril, for children. But as we have seen, it only takes a few steps and a small dose of parental supervision to start your children down a safe onramp to the Internet superhighway.

So Where Do You Want to Go with Your Kids?

It is important for parents to get involved with kids and computers. First off, if you do not get involved, kids will have little to no exposure until school, and from that point forward you will be a "divided family" in that you will do your thing and your kid will do theirs on the computer. Of course this is not where we want to end up! And so by getting involved you are making sure your child has as much of a "leg up" as any other child. Secondly, your getting involved is key to any other challenge of parenting. Interaction will drastically increase the likelihood of your developing the competence to oversee effectively.

I am a fairly tech-savvy person. I have designed webpages, some of the graphics you see in this book, and respond to hundreds of e-mails a day for a living. But when it came to taking my kid places on the Internet, I must admit I have often been stumped! And it is for no other reason than because there are so many possibilities. That, and I did have a lot of time to spend finding good places to go for a five-year-old. Because of the sheer size of the Internet, parents are often quite intimidated as to what guidance to give to their kids online.

The place to start is with a pencil and a piece of paper. Forget about the Internet, just write down the ten things your kids like the most. For example, if I were to do this for my older son, the list might begin like this:

1. *Thomas the Tank Engine*
2. Ice Cream
3. Trucks
4. When Is It Going to Snow Again
5. Swimming

Search Engines for Kids

When you begin to explore the Internet with your child, don't use "normal" web search engines like Yahoo and Google. Use kids' versions instead. These tend to filter out inappropriate sites and often only list kid-specific sites. These include:

1. Yahooligans: *www.yahooligans.com*
2. KidsClick!: *www.kidsclick.org*
3. Looksmart Kids: *search.netnanny.com*
4. Ask Jeeves for Kids: *www.ajkids.com*

Some of the things you put on your list might just be passing interests of the moment (like when is it going to snow again). But that is okay; you can redo your list at any time. This list serves, of course, as your browsing list for you to explore with your child. Make each topic a single session online, or have it even span multiple sessions.

Another strategy is to make a list of sites that you want to visit with your kid. This not only includes the usual websites from TV shows, but also the websites of museums, kids' musical groups, and your child's own elementary school and library.

Video Games

Video games are a topic that will be dealt with in detail in the next chapter. For now, though, our task is to learn how to filter the medium. For television we learned about television ratings and how to use them to filter our televisions from potentially harmful content. For the Internet, we learned to put filtering software in place. In both we learned that a healthy dose of oversight goes a long way.

Like television, video games have their own set of ratings. The only problem is, there is no "VG-chip" for video games. The only possible filtering is from your understanding the ratings system and limiting what your children play by selectively buying appropriate games and avoiding ones you deem unacceptable.

Video Game Ratings: Is That Game Okay to Play?

If you thought television ratings were a little complicated, that is because you did not know there were ratings for video games! Still, once read they are fairly easy to understand:

EC—Early Childhood: These games have content that may be suitable for ages 3 and older. Titles in this category contain no material that parents would find inappropriate.

 E—Everyone: These games have content that may be suitable for ages 6 and older. Titles in this category may contain minimal cartoon, fantasy, or mild violence and/or infrequent use of mild language.

 E10+—Everyone Age Ten and older: These games have content that may be suitable for ages 10 and older. Titles in this category may contain more cartoon, fantasy or mild violence, mild language, and/or minimal suggestive themes.

 T—Teen: These games have content that may be suitable for ages 13 and older. Titles in this category may contain violence, suggestive themes, crude humor, minimal blood, simulated gambling, and/or infrequent use of strong language.

 M—Mature: These games have content that may be suitable for ages 17 and older. Titles in this category may contain intense violence, blood and gore, sexual content, and/or strong language.

 AO—Adults Only: These games have content that should only be played by persons 18 years and older. Titles in this category may include prolonged scenes of intense violence and/or graphic sexual content and nudity.

The ESRB rating icons are registered trademarks of the Entertainment Software Association

Games may also have an "RP" rating which means "rating pending," and companies are allowed to sell games so long as they have been submitted to the board that reviews video games (the Entertainment Software Rating Board, or ESRB).

Alcohol Reference—Reference to and/or images of alcoholic beverages
Animated Blood—Discolored and/or unrealistic depictions of blood
Blood—Depictions of blood
Blood and Gore—Depictions of blood or the mutilation of body parts
Cartoon Violence—Violent actions involving cartoon-like situations and characters; may include violence where a character is unharmed after the action has been inflicted
Comic Mischief—Depictions or dialogue involving slapstick or suggestive humor
Crude Humor—Depictions or dialogue involving vulgar antics, including "bathroom" humor
Drug Reference—Reference to and/or images of illegal drugs
Fantasy Violence—Violent actions of a fantasy nature, involving human or nonhuman characters in situations easily distinguishable from real life
Intense Violence—Graphic and realistic-looking depictions of physical conflict; may involve extreme and/or realistic blood, gore, weapons, and depictions of human injury and death
Language—Mild to moderate use of profanity
Lyrics—Mild references to profanity, sexuality, violence, alcohol, or drug use in music
Mature Humor—Depictions or dialogue involving "adult" humor, including sexual references
Nudity—Graphic or prolonged depictions of nudity
Partial Nudity—Brief and/or mild depictions of nudity
Real Gambling—Player can gamble, including betting or wagering real cash or currency
Sexual Content—Nonexplicit depictions of sexual behavior, possibly including partial nudity
Sexual Themes—References to sex or sexuality
Sexual Violence—Depictions of rape or other violent sexual acts
Simulated Gambling—Player can gamble without betting or wagering real cash or currency
Strong Language—Explicit and/or frequent use of profanity
Strong Lyrics—Explicit and/or frequent references to profanity, sex, violence, alcohol, or drug use in music
Strong Sexual Content—Explicit and/or frequent depictions of sexual behavior, possibly including nudity
Suggestive Themes—Mild provocative references or materials
Tobacco Reference—Reference to and/or images of tobacco products
Use of Drugs—The consumption or use of illegal drugs
Use of Alcohol—The consumption of alcoholic beverages
Use of Tobacco—The consumption of tobacco products
Violence—Scenes involving aggressive conflict; may contain bloodless dismemberment
Violent References—References to violent acts

When a content descriptor is preceded by the term 'Mild,' it conveys low frequency intensity or severity of the content it modifies. Content descriptors are not intended to be a listing of every type of content one might encounter in the course of playing a game. Online-enabled games carry the notice "Online Interactions Not Rated by the ESRB." This notice warns those who intend to play the game online about possible exposure to chat (text, audio, video) or other types of user-generated content (e.g., maps, skins) that have not been considered in the ESRB rating assignment.

Now that we understand the ratings, what they should be allowed to play at this age and what we need to start thinking about in the future. If I had to sum up the impact of electronic media in this age, it would be this: Enjoy it. These first three chapters were your training. You are now a master at understanding how to control content, from television to the Internet to video games. This was your training camp. Now, your child is ready to become a preteen. And if they say that today's 50 is yesterday's 40, then surely today's preteen is yesterday's middle school child.

Video Games for Early Elementary School Children

Video Games can be educational, just like computer games can. Here are some sites that review and rate games for age appropriateness:

- **Love to Know.com:** A small site with a small list of approved games for kids. *videogames.lovetoknow.com*
- **National Institute on Media and the Family:** An organization with an eye out for video game violence and other inappropriate content. *www.mediafamily.org* (search for their video game report card)
- **Entertainment Software Rating Board:** The board that provides the official ratings of all video games. *www.esrb.org*
- **IGN Entertainment:** A good site just to see what a game is all about, but which doesn't include ratings. *www.ign.com*

Put simply, today's preteens are doing things we never dreamed of. Kids seem to continually to enter the adult world at a younger and younger age, whether or not they are truly prepared for it. As parents it is our job is to prepare them for adulthood. Your child is about to confront media in all its glory, good and bad. Television programming for adults. Chat partners who might not be who they seem. Video games that commonly show decapitations. So on to the next chapter. But do not worry, you are ready.

CHAPTER 4 CHEAT SHEET

TELEVISION

KEY CONCERN	Shows for your kids are starting to get more and more violent.
REMEDY	Low consumption, interactive parenting.
KEY NEW SKILL	Using the ratings system and V-chip controls to limit content.
SPECIAL TOPIC	Be sure to limit adult content and be cautious introducing the news.

COMPUTERS AND INTERNET

KEY NEW SKILL	Setting up filtering software and a safe public workspace for your computer.
SECONDARY SKILL	Finding great websites and games for kids that are interactive and educational.

VIDEO GAMES

KEY NEW SKILL	Learning the video game rating system.
KEY CONCERN	Overuse.

Preteens

WHILE CHILDREN ARE born with some ability to fight off infection, and are built to withstand a wide range of bumps and bruises as they learn to physically master their bodies, it does not seem fair that they are not pre-equipped to deal with media in any way whatsoever. In fact, some higher-order thinking abilities are required to understand the point of commercials. It takes a good dose of intellect to understand fantasy violence is just that—fantasy. And it takes experience and age to really understand the "unreality" of media, where everyone appears rich and beautiful, and bullets are more bountiful than people (remember the A-Team?).

So few parents take the time to help their children live with and understand the media as they do other integral aspects of life. Parents themselves find media so easy to use that they might think, what is there to teach? You just turn on the TV and go! And as we have briefly discussed, other parents may avoid such issues because they already feel "outmastered" with regard to the Internet and other emerging media technologies.

For most parents, even if they realize that it is nearly as important to teach their kids about media as it is to recite their ABCs, well, few really know where to start. While this chapter will continue to teach you how to raise your children in the media age, there is an important shift. In past chapters, the message was protection. Not allowing infants to watch television. Not allowing children to view violent programming or play violent videogames. Not allowing kids to have access to Internet sites that have offensive material, and so on.

Now, though, it is fast becoming time to move from protection to inoculation. Why the shift? I hope I am not the first to break this to you, but you are losing control. You may *think* you are not, or maybe you are all too aware. But the fact is: a) You cannot oversee your children's media use all the time, and b) They are increasingly becoming experts at media and thus able to strike out on their own with regard to television, video games, and the Internet.

This chapter will continue to review the research regarding television, video games, the Internet and computers, advertising, and music. In addition, the conversation will turn more and more to inoculation rather than prevention, since as parents we increasingly have less ability to control, but at the same time, our children are gaining more and more of an ability to understand. Instill children with strong moral values and they will, most likely, become moral people. And likewise, the more you instill a child with an understanding of how media can manipulate them and provide them with a very distorted mirror of the real world, the better you can protect them from the potentially harmful effects media may have.

Body Image and the Media

Ah yes, preteens. The age where looks go from meaning nothing to meaning everything. By this age many kids are already preoccupied with looks. But now that preoccupation often becomes an obsession!

Kids tend to go to two places to figure out how they should look. First, they look to their peers and older siblings and classmates. Second, they look to mass media. They certainly don't go to parents! If you doubt the power of media in promoting certain looks and fashions, you need not look any further than your own adolescences. In the 1980s, how did we learn to love leg warmers, berets, big hair, and mullets? Trust me, only the media has the power to persuade us to make so many terrible fashion choices!

Unfortunately, the power of the media does not stop at "fashion image." Indeed, there is a long tradition of scientific research showing that the media also affects what we want to be in terms of "body image" as well.

Simply put, people on television, and in the media in general, are beautiful. But most importantly, our collective, cultural definition of what beautiful really is, is pretty much based on what the media defines it to be. Take for example a study by Sypeck and colleagues of cover girls in popular fashion/women's magazines like *Cosmopolitan*, *Glamour*, *Mademoiselle*, and *Vogue*. What do you think a typical young male teenager's image of the "perfect" woman was circa 1959? What comes to most people's minds is a woman in the one-piece-boy-shorts swimming suit, a bit buxom (but naturally so), curly hair, and by today's standards, a bit heavier. How about the image of women, in the mind of that same teenage boy today? Fit, thin, probably still buxom (though perhaps not naturally so), and long hair, often minky-straight.

The Importance of Weight

It is probably no surprise, then, that research by Garner on the image portrayed by models in these magazines changed over the course of fifty years, from 1959 to 1999. First, the models have become much thinner. In fact, a related study of *Playboy* playmate models found a substantial decrease in Body Mass Index of the models from 1953 to 2001. Body Mass Index, a simple numeric measure of a person's "fatness" or "thinness," ranges from about sixteen to the high thirties. The average American has a BMI of twenty-eight. As is evident in the chart below, *Playboy* models are far below average. In addition to having a lower BMI, the study also found that the hip to waist ratio became larger, meaning the hourglass shape is more pronounced today.

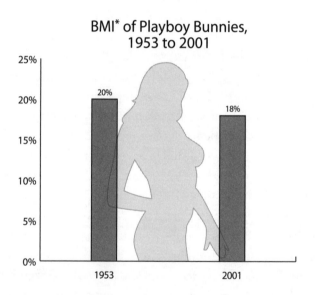

BMI* of Playboy Bunnies, 1953 to 2001

Source: Garner   * Body Mass Index

Other studies like those by Hawkins and others consistently find that people in the mass media (actors, actresses, spokespersons, and models) are on average fifteen percent thinner than the average American.

So the "perfect" woman has become thin to the point that the majority of women alive today could not possibly attain. And they are commonly airbrushed, thinned (commonly by stretching out the legs of women with photo manipulation software), and re-colored to maximize their appeal. And it is not just models who portray such perfect images. One has only to look at reality shows such as *Survivor* and *The Apprentice* to realize that even "real" people in the media are hand-selected on looks first and personality second. These "real" people are not average looking, by any reasonable standard.

So the fact that media show many bodies that attain the "thin ideal," and very few average body types (or greater than average), one has to ask, does it matter? Obviously, we like to look at good looking people, and thus, the media gives people what they want. What harm is there in that?

The Effects of the Thin Ideal

Researchers tend to find effects large and small, no pun intended. First is simply the internalization of the thin ideal, that is, the degree to which preteens, teenagers, and even adults simply internalize the media's thin ideal. What do researchers mean by internalized the thin ideal? Specifically, they mean that such people are convinced that the only way to be popular, successful, and satisfied with life in general is to attain a body comparable to those seen in the media. Thus, accepting the thin ideal image is the "gateway" to potentially more harmful effects of the thin ideal. And indeed, people are more likely to try extreme dieting and exercise, and even the abuse of laxatives and vomiting, to become as thin as possible if they believe in the thin ideal. The thin ideal is even linked to eating disorders such as bulimia and anorexia nervosa. But even if a child does not develop an eating disorder, who wants a child to live their life constantly unhappy in his or her own skin?

Being constantly bombarded with thin ideal images also impacts self-esteem and increases what scientists call "negative mood states," including depression, anxiety, and insecurity, as well as our satisfaction with our own bodies.

The typical body-image experiment involves splitting a set of people into two groups. One group will see a range of programming, stories and advertising with thin ideal characters, and the other group will see the same media, but with average-looking actors, actresses, and models. Those who are exposed to the thin ideal images are often found to be twice as likely to develop depressive thoughts, low self-esteem, and of course, dissatisfaction of their own body images. These are not small effects, like we found with early television and attention problems; these are significant effects.

A study by Schutz and Paxton of adolescent girls found that those with the most body dissatisfaction were more likely to report negative interactions with their friends. Those include the general social anxiety and social insecurity, as well as the more specific concepts of alienation and conflict amongst friends. For those with significant body dissatisfaction and symptoms of eating disorders, these negative aspects were far more present than they were with teenagers without these symptoms. Acceptance of the thin ideal hurts friendships and other relationships.

And finally, there is the most dangerous potential effect of all: feeling the need to binge diet because of the thin ideal. Some may even develop eating disorders. Indeed, when researchers study people with a pre-diagnosed eating disorder, those that were exposed to thin ideal images were far more dissatisfied with their own image, had lower self esteem, and had far more negative emotions like depression, anger, and anxiety, than people without eating disorders.

Of course, it is important to remember that there is a three-way link here: Media exposure leading to body dissatisfaction, and the body dissatisfaction leading to a host of negative health and psychological outcomes. What can you do? Communicate with your child about the impact of media on how they feel about themselves. In this case, knowledge can truly be power as understanding the source of the problem is an important step (and as a reminder, media are not the only source of body dissatisfaction, so if your preteen or teen seems uncomfortable in his or her own skin, look for other sources as well).

The message of the above sections is that it is time to start getting into the practice of teaching your children about media. One place a parent can start is with a discussion about the nature of actors, actresses, and models, and why they do what they do, who they are, that they do not represent the average American on many levels, and that even they need help from the air brushers and personal trainers to look the

It's Not Just for Girls Anymore

Early on, the research tradition on body image all seemed to focus primarily on women. But as more and more men in the media show off more and more skin and muscles than ever before, the research literature has quickly caught up.

This is not a women-only problem. Researchers like Baird and Grieve have found that both genders are affected. Studies of preadolescents find that thirty-five percent of both girls *and* boys are dissatisfied with their bodies. However, once they become adolescents, the boys become less dissatisfied, and, of those who are dissatisfied, only half of them actually want to lose weight. Interestingly, half of preadolescent boys don't want to lose weight; they want to get bigger. In the mind of a preadolescent boy, it is thought, the desire for bigger muscles outweighs the value of simply being thin.

way they do. Be clear on what impact body image can have on your preteen. Let them know, they are too good for that. The message, in short: Don't let media tell your child what to think about themselves.

Despite Wanting to Get Thin, Are Kids Just Getting More Overweight?

If there is one area of media research where people seem to disagree the most, it is in the answer to this question. Many authors who have written on this topic have been convinced this has to be the case. After all, if children are watching a lot of television, then they are spending a lot of time being sedentary, rather than out playing in the yard, right? Well, the problem with this thinking is that it assumes children would be spending time playing physically if they were not stuck in front of the TV. Not true. Studies are in fact mixed. Some find no difference in the time spent in physical activity and play for kids who watch a lot of television compared to those who watch only a little. Other studies find a difference, but it tends to be quite small. On average, we can say that less television does not necessarily mean more physical activity and playtime.

Nevertheless, this does not mean that heavy use of television, video games, and computers by your preteen will not lead to obesity. The question of obesity is a complex one that is not easily explained away by over-watching television. It is unclear if it is the television-sitting that is making such children fat or whether they are watching television because they are already overweight and not interested in physical activity.

Overall, the attempt to link obesity and heavy media use continues on, with a history of contradictory effects, or none at all. However, you should still remain vigilant. If your child is spending four or more hours each day using television, video games, and the computer, you ought to be rightly concerned that they get out and interact more with the outside world. They may or may not lose weight, but surely they will live a more active childhood.

Computers and the Internet

To this point in their lives, the use of the Internet by your child has, at least for the typical child, been a bit like dabbling one's toe into the pool. A little bit of this (chat) and perhaps a little bit of that (e-mail), with a bit more of web browsing.

But often during the preteen years, all sorts of online activities begin in earnest. The children are prepared to discover sites related to their hobbies and interests, often without parental guidance. From school alone they will be conducting research. The encyclopedias you and I started with in the school library? They are more often than not now accessed electronically. You might remember that pen pal your teacher encouraged you to have? Today's Internet is like steroids for pen-paling. It is so much easier to communicate great distances, thanks to the Internet.

Let's take a look at what your preteen is likely doing on online: As the charts on the following page show, Internet use grows substantially as children grow through the preteen years. Internet browsing quickly moves from having mom and dad in control to mom and dad having what at times seems like no control at all! And use of the Internet is no longer just educational, as the preteen learns to find information on products, though still very few of them are directly making a purchase (and for reasons we will discuss shortly, it is a good thing this percentage has yet to reach double digits).

Preteens are becoming communication experts. E-mail, cell phones, instant messages, and chat rooms all quickly

Preteen Computer Users: What Do They Use it For?

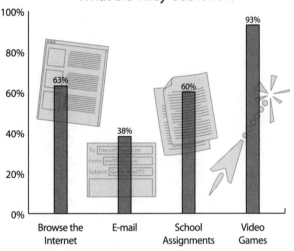

Source: Pew Internet and the American Life Project

Teen Internet Users: What Do They Use it For?

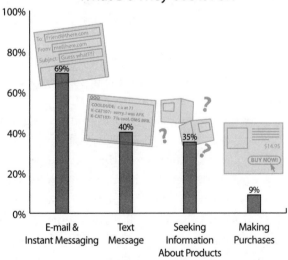

Source: Pew Internet and the American Life Project

become simple means of communication, each with their own peculiarities. For perhaps this reason, your preteen will learn to turn to one form of communication versus another based on her needs. Indeed, studies show preteens increasingly turning to instant messages for gossip but text messaging for flirting or making plans.

But with great power comes great responsibility. The potential to receive harm or to cause harm is very real in the online world. Thus online harm is no less painful than its real world equivalents.

Cyber Bullying

Unfortunately, bullying has made its way from the schoolyard to the Internet. About two-thirds of teenagers say they have been bullied in person, while one-third has been a victim of online bullying.

What is online bullying? It is the reception of threatening messages, the willful sharing of private information to hurt someone psychologically, be it text or graphics (like embarrassing photos), or the spreading of rumors using electronic communication.

When one thinks of play yard bullying, the stereotypical image is of a boy being roughed-up by the big kid on the block. But online, it's the girls who take the brunt of the attack, as about 38 percent of girls report cyber bullying compared to 26 percent of boys.

Cyber bullying can be an annoyance, but sometimes it is much, much more. Threatened harm can become physical harm. And in some ways, the psychological harm created by bullying can be far more acute online, because it is so much easier to take something public, and for many people to "witness" the bullying. Take an example from a focus group conducted by the Pew Internet and American Life Project, where the anatomy class "geek" takes the brunt of the attack. One girl in his class writes: "He always wants to work in our group and I hate it. And we started this thing, some girl in my class started this I Hate [Name] MySpace thing. So everybody in school goes on it to comment bad things about this boy." That is certainly not something you want your child to do, or to happen to your child.

Percent of Online Kids Who Have Been Bullied by the...

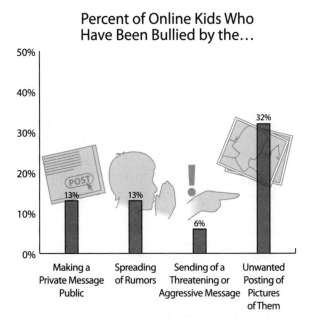

Source: Pew Internet and American Life Project

And while we are on the topic of MySpace, it is important to understand that if your child is connected to e-mail, chat rooms, and the like, they are much more likely to be a victim of cyber bullying, as the majority of cyber bullying occurs in these public spaces. Nearly twice as many teens who use a social network site will be cyber bullied than teens that do not use such sites.

Of course, there is *cyber* bullying, and then there is cyber *bullying*. Small-talk gossip may be an annoyance, but hate-crime bullying, online harassment, and threats of physical violence are nothing to take lightly. Harassment is defined as threats to assault or harm a youth, their family, friends, or property, or an otherwise blatant attempt to humiliate. Generally, preteens are not as much of a target as older teenagers, and as you can see, there is cause for concern, even in the younger age categories:

Harassment of Online Kids by Age

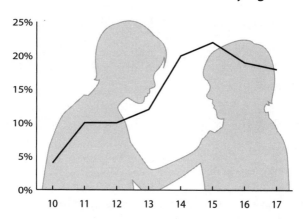

Source: Crimes Against Children Research Center

Who is the perpetrator of harassment? Mostly, it's your children's peers. How does it impact your preteen or teen? About a third report being extremely upset by the episode, and one in five reports having been very afraid when it occurred.

One problem with cyber bullying, like other forms of bullying, is that only about half of teenagers that are bullied tell their parents. Second, most parents have no idea what to do with the information. Going to the source, that is, the parents of the bully, can often lead to disastrous results. The bully will have all the more reason to bully.

What Can You Do if Your Preteen is Being Cyber-Bullied?

The first step is again, inoculation. In this case, what I mean by that is that by getting the information to your teen or preteen first that you know what cyber bullying is and they should feel safe in telling you if it happens to them will maximize the chance you are not in the half of all parents who are clueless when bullying happens to their kids. And if we can all take off our "my kid would never do that!" hats for a second, let's realize that such a talk also gives us the opportunity to tell our children we would never allow them to bully another.

Okay then, what should be done when cyber bullying occurs? Experts suggest a few courses of action. First, the best course of action is no reaction—your child should not respond to the bullying at all. Second, make sure you save all evidence, in case it's needed. Learn how to take a screen shot of what you see on your monitor (this is quite easy on a PC or a Mac) so that you can save or print the evidence.

One problem with cyber bulling is that often it can be anonymous. However, if the bullying is threatening to harm and you are sufficiently concerned this might be a crime or lead to one, there are tracking alternatives the police can enact. You should contact the police if there are specific threats of violence, or extortion, or if you witness child pornography or a hate crime.

And of course, there still remains the decision of whether to contact the bully's parents. In many cases, a parent will be in disbelief that their little sweetheart could do such a thing. Other parents are all too aware and, for various reasons, do not intervene. Most experts recommend that you find whatever information you can about the family before you make a decision whether to intervene. Some suggest saying you found the bullying on the computer and your child is completely unaware that you are contacting them (whether this is true or not), to best protect your child from negative backlash. Finally, it is recommended that you contact the parents in writing, and with proof. Do so as plain-spoken as you can—just the facts. Simply ask them to do what they can to stop the bullying.

A last avenue of recourse is your child's school. Many schools today are part of anti-bullying campaigns and have protocols in place when bullying does occur. Indeed, many states now require all schools to have a formal program.

Finally, make sure your kid understands that they are not alone. You are there to support them. Let them know the facts; that two thirds of kids get bullied at one time of their lives. It may seem to them they have been singled out as a victim for a reason. Very often this is not the case, and even if it is, remember, so too are many, many of their classmates.

Online Predators

Let's play with some numbers, using data from the Crimes Against Children Research Center. Say your preteen is in the sixth grade along with one hundred other sixth graders. How many received a sexual advance or solicitation on the Internet in the last year? The answer is, twenty of them. And, it is estimated, at least three of these led to an aggressive solicitation such as a request to meet somewhere, to call on a telephone, or to send mail (regular, USPS mail like a gift or letter).

When you add up all the ten to seventeen-year-olds out there, about thirty-four million, you are talking over a million children who are getting aggressive sexual solicitations from strangers over the Internet every year. At any one moment, there are as many as 50,000 online predators "working" online. And because they are afraid their parents will ban them from computer access, only about one in ten of the children receiving these solicitations tell their parents about it (though at least one in six do tell some other adult about it).

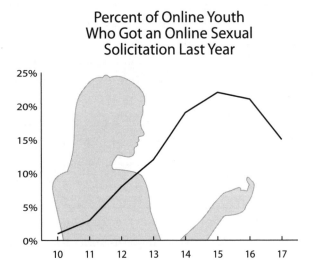

Percent of Online Youth Who Got an Online Sexual Solicitation Last Year

Source: Crimes Against Children Research Center

As the chart above illustrates, most solicitations occur during the teenage years. But the unwanted sexual advances start at about ten years of age. Two thirds of the targets of these unwanted advances are girls. And while most targets were in their teenage years, preteens report being much more distressed by the advances.

Importantly, nearly all sexual solicitations come from strangers whom children met at least once already online, be it through a chat room or e-mail. Most solicitors are young; in fact, below the age of eighteen and only about one in five are women. It is really important to understand one statistic above all others, and that is that one-third of teenagers say they have talked to a stranger online about meeting in person. So please, do not assume that "my kids would never . . ." Instead, take the approach that you can never be too safe.

Your Prevention Program for Cyber Predators

Here are ten "rules of the road" developed by protectkids.com. Share these with your kids and make sure they understand them:

1. Never give out personal information such as name, address, and phone number.
2. Never meet anyone in person that you met online.
3. Do not use chat rooms.
4. Never give out schedule information: where you will be, and whether and when your parents are home (not even to friends . . . tell them in person or on the phone).
5. Never respond to new people you meet online. Have a parent review that person's request first.
6. Never go to an online area that costs money without your parent's permission.
7. Never send a picture of yourself over the Internet.
8. Never buy products and/or use a credit card online without your parent's permission.
9. Always immediately end any online experience that makes you uncomfortable.
10. Always tell mom and dad about something that was upsetting to you online.

What do predators say? Many ask their targets to "cyber," which is short for cybersex, which is a chat room discussion of a sexual nature that is designed to turn on the predator. Other predators try to get "in" by asking about measurements, which later leads to questions about what the target does sexually or statements of what the predator likes to do sexually. The goal of this "foreplay" is often a personal meeting. Does your child ever use chat rooms (not the Club Penguin variety but its more mature cousins)? If so, there is a twenty percent chance they have been approached by a pedophile.

What can you do to help your child avoid predators? Talk to your children about online "friends." Make sure they understand they are strangers. Predation never starts off with a sexual solicitation. Predation begins by getting the child to talk about their hobbies, interests, etc. Predators know they need to warm children up into a comfortable relationship first. Make sure your children understand how predators work.

Also, you can oversee your child's Internet interactions. Use the monitoring features of your Internet filtering device. Screen all incoming mail to your child to make sure you

Popping Some Questions

If you ever suspect a problem with online predation, here are some questions protectkids.com suggests you ask your children:

1. Have you seen any pornographic pictures?
2. Has anyone online talked dirty to you?
3. Have you met anyone online whom you don't know?
4. Has anyone asked you for personal information?
5. Has anyone asked to meet you in person?

know who they are getting mail from (both e-mail and regular mail). The same is true of phone calls. Respect their privacy, but oversee nevertheless. Strike a balanced medium. If you really think there is a problem, you can go so far as to disallow the use of chat rooms, though I do not recommend this as children will find a way (indeed, a recent study found that nearly ninety percent of children say they could go to a chat room without their parents knowledge).

Getting Addicted to the Internet

A final caution that is best prevented with inoculation: Internet addiction. The sad truth is that as many as three percent of all Internet users could be classified as being addicted to the Internet. What is Internet addiction? In short, you are online for a long time, and when you are not, your thoughts are dominated by the last online session or thinking about the next session you will have. Like other forms of addiction, Internet addiction can be broken down into key elements:

1. *Salience*: Using the Internet becomes the most important recreational activity in one's life.
2. *Mood Modification:* The Internet becomes a primary method of relieving bad moods and elevating good moods.
3. *Tolerance:* More and more time on the Internet is necessary to get the same type of mood modification than before.
4. *Withdrawal Symptoms:* NOT being on the Internet creates an uneasy feeling.
5. *Conflict:* The Internet is the activity of choice even in situations where this causes conflict with other activities, including school work, sleep, and for adults and older teenagers, work.
6. *Relapse:* Periods of being offline are followed by a heightened need to reconnect.

While some scholars debate whether people can truly get addicted to the Internet or just addicted to certain activities on the Internet (games, gambling, sex and pornography, or addiction in developing online relationships), I think the point here is that there is certainly a point at which there is too much of a good thing, and the Internet is no exception.

Some think that the addiction often surfaces during the college years to young adulthood, but there are certainly documented cases of abuse by preteens and teenagers as well.

Of all the dangers in this book, this is likely the least prevalent among children. However, it is clear that you should not be allowing excessive time on the Internet any more than you have allowed excessive use of television. If your child seems to be asking to go online more so than any other activity, talk to her to understand why she wants to go online, and if her requests and subsequent actual time on the Internet becomes an issue, talk to her about it and mediate time spent online.

Video Games

Pong. Space Invaders. Galaga. Donkey Kong. Remember the glory days? Where home video games were barely adequate, yet captured kid's imaginations with their terrible graphics, and where the video arcade used to house, oh, about ten games? Today, video arcades need to decide what to have—there are too many choices. But that is nothing compared to the difference between today's home video games and the home video games of old. Today's video games leave little to the imagination, simply because they don't have to. The graphics are too good, the processors too fast. We have gone from a nation that in the mid-1980s had probably fewer than 100 games available, to one where thousands and thousands of titles are available.

Nearly all children report playing video games (ninety-two percent in 2002 according to the Kaiser Family Foundation). About two-thirds of preteens live in a home that owns a video game system of some kind. And half of these households has a video game system in their kid's bedroom. Video game use peaks in the preteen and middle school years; on average a half an hour a day is spent playing games. Among those who actually play video games regularly, that number increases to just over an hour a day. Just about one in every five preteen boys spends an hour EVERY day playing video games.

Action and sports video games are just about equally popular amongst preteenagers. Adventure games are popular as well. Nine out of every ten video games contains some form of violent content. Four out of every five human characters in video games is male. It is perhaps unsurprising, then, that twice as many boys play video games as girls.

Not all games and gaming are bad. In fact a number of positive effects have been found with regard to video games. As mentioned a few chapters back, video games can teach problem solving skills, hand-eye coordination, spatial skills, and spatial visualization. Some studies find girls lagging behind boys in a number of these measures, and video game use brings them quickly up to speed. Of course, when it comes to video games, for every one nice thing said about them, there must be ten negative comments, if not one hundred. And it is not just because adults don't get it. The fears are real and parents should understand them if they want to do everything they can to protect their children from harmful media.

Video Game Violence

Did you know that a game like *Halo 3* will make more money than the vast majority of movies that will be released this year? The feedback on the Internet about this game and the comments about it tend toward the extreme. One parent stands amazed that today's kids cannot seem to plan ahead more than an hour or two, yet for months they have been saving and saving for this game, and now that the game is finally out, they are playing and playing. Another source of amazement: Kids, with their vaunted limited attention spans, are able to play this game for literally hours on end without need, seemingly, for drink or rest. Other commentators call the game "America's new crack," saying essentially that it is no wonder America is going downhill with teens so addicted to such games.

Surprisingly few comments said a word about the violence of the game. My guess is, in comparison to other games nowadays, the violence in *Halo 3* is pretty much normal. But then again, I suppose that is the point: When violence becomes normal then what does the normal kid look like?

The more that the effects of violence in video games are studied, the larger the effects appear to be. These effects appear widespread. Below is a very quick summary of what violent video games can do.

Video games have been found to be linked to holding aggressive norms, though the evidence is limited on whether this leads to an aggressive attributional style. What this means is that researchers compare children who play video games to those who do not, or at least, do so at low levels. They ask all these children a number of questions, including whether it is totally okay, somewhat okay, not really okay, or not at all okay to kick and push a person when one is really angry, or to destroy something belonging to another as an act of revenge, or to threaten to beat someone up who has made you angry. Sure enough, on average, people who play violent video games are more likely to agree that these behaviors are okay. That's probably not what you want your kids to think.

Similarly, research like that conducted by Karhe and Moller show that violent video games have been found to shorten the fuse. Simply put, kids who play violent video games become more and more primed for aggressive thoughts and actions, such that when a situation presents itself where both aggressive and nonaggressive solutions may be pursued, it is more likely that the child takes the aggressive course of action.

Yet another impact of violent video games, as with most graphic entertainment, is desensitization. Desensitization is a

A Short List of Effects from Video Game Violence

Scientists have found a seemingly unlimited number of ways video games can be harmful to your health.

1. *Hostile attributional style:* Taking ambiguous events, such as something said in conversation, and interpreting it as aggressive or hostile (yes, we have all been there with our significant others!).
2. *Automatic aggressiveness:* When people more closely associate themselves with negative personality traits than with positive ones.
3. *Desensitization:* The more violence you see, the less it quickens your pulse, and the less you care about it.
4. *School performance:* Enough said.
5. *Aggressive behaviors:* Includes both psychological (arguments, etc.) and physical (fights, etc.).
6. *Aggressive Cognition:* Essentially, thinking aggressive thoughts.
7. *Helping Behavior:* You guessed it, the amount to which we reach out to others (obviously, the thought here is the violent video games make you a less helpful person).
8. *Aggressive Norms:* Thinking that aggressive behavior is socially normal.

fun concept to explore with my research methods class. To demonstrate desensitization, I play a video clip from a horror movie and have half of my students take the pulse of the other half of the students. Then I replay the clip, and those who got their pulse taken the first time take the pulse of the other students on this second run. Sure enough, the pulses the second time through are dramatically lower. Scary scenes just aren't as scary the second time around because you know what is coming.

Now, repeat this experiment every day for ten years. Do you think violence in the media might have an impact on how we feel about violence, and how much empathy we feel toward others? Sure enough, study after study, like those conducted by Funk and colleagues, have found that we have become a society where those of us who consume a lot of media are disproportionately less empathetic and more desensitized to violence.

One of the problems of violent video games is not about the games itself, but about the age group that seems to love them the most: adolescents. More than a few studies have found the impact on children in grades seven though ten to be worse than on adults who, we think, are more mature and thus better able to deal with the fantasy violence of the games. In fact, adolescents who play a lot of video games not only do poorer in school, but they also report getting into more fights, arguments with teachers, and are more hostile overall. Of more concern still is emerging evidence that video game violence is a "downward spiral," meaning the more you play, the worse your behavior can become.

Violent video games not only increase aggressive thoughts and even actions in our preteens and teenagers. They also can reduce a number of positive behaviors, including the coveted prosocial behavior you worked on in earlier chapters. Violent video games don't just increase aggression; they decrease the degree to which we care about others.

Of course, it is not just boys who get to have all the fun. There has been some suggestion that girls are not affected as strongly by the aggression-inducing effects of video games. Certainly, boys play violent video games much more often than girls. And to some degree, the girls are not impacted as much because they do not wish to be the lead character in the game as much as boys do. But recently it has been realized that this is very much in large part because there are so few characters for females to idealize. But nowadays, there are more and more female characters in the most violent of games. And sure enough, studies find that girls that identify with these female gaming characters are affected most by the violent content of these games. So unfortunately, when

The Video Game Star Is My Hero

It is natural for kids to fantasize about being the character in a movie or a video game. But interestingly, it might not be such a good thing for your child to wish too much to be the lead character in a violent video game. In one experiment conducted by Konijn, Bijvank and Bushman, adolescents were put into a testing task where they were permitted to sound a loud noise toward their partner in the task. Those who played violent video games were more likely to blast their partner with a noise so loud it could potentially cause hearing damage. But if this was not bad enough, the researchers found that those who not only played the violent video game but also wished the most that they were like the lead character in the games blasted the loudest of noises, despite the noise clearly hurting their partner.

it comes to violent video games, it is no longer a man's (or boy's) world.

What Can You Do Regarding Violent Video Games?

So what can be done to mitigate the negative impact of violent video games? Of course, the first step is to either completely disallow certain games or to limit their use. The choice here must fall to each household, as parents must weigh the potential backlash of a complete ban (and after all, they will probably just go to someone else's house to play such games anyway, outside of your watch) with the mitigated impact of moderate use of these games.

But regardless of your decision, remember this: the more you communicate with your child, the less violent video games appear to induce aggression. Overall, there is no known "magic potion" to curtail the impact of violent video games. The best strategy is to understand the impact violent video games can have, and to find ways to communicate these effects to your child and thus provide them a rationale for why you need to limit exposure to such games. If outright limiting of titles proves difficult, be sure to try what is perhaps an easier road, which is to allow the titles of choice by your children, but then to limit the number of hours per day your children are allowed to play any games whatsoever.

Getting Out of Hand: Video Game Addiction

Earlier in this chapter we discussed the possibility of having Internet use mirror the behaviors of other addictions. A similar concern has been found in video games. Salguero and Moran found that persons that used video games excessively mirrored the dependence syndrome found in other addicts. How many people get addicted to video games? The answer is somewhat unclear. A survey conducted by an online gaming magazine found that twelve percent of the participants could be qualified as addicted. These gamers played games an excessive number of hours per day, exhibited substantially higher expectations of relief when gaming, and craved video games significantly more when not playing.

One thing is certain: video game addiction is real. It usually occurs once one is away from the limiting constraints of mom, dad, and school. After all, it is difficult for a preteen to get away with five hours a day of video game use, unless the parent is totally out to lunch (and lets be honest, some parents are). But the seeds of addiction often start in the preteen years, so it is important for parents to recognize the signs. Studies say to look for falling academic achievement and achievement in other areas of life as well. It is important to make these points here because of all the addictions, video game addiction certainly gets the least amount of attention. But if your child begins to exhibit the following behaviors (as provided by the National Institute on Media and the Family) you should take action:

1. Most of nonschool hours are spent on the computer or playing video games.
2. Falling asleep in school.
3. Not keeping up with assignments.
4. Worsening grades.
5. Lying about computer or video game use.
6. Choosing to use the computer or play video games, rather than see friends.
7. Dropping out of other social groups (clubs or sports).
8. Irritable when not playing a video game or when not on the computer.

The key is to immediately begin to curtail video game use within the home. This is a behavior that is best caught early. Video games should not be allowed until all homework is complete, as well as chores and perhaps some mandatory quiet/reading time. Enroll your child in activities that take him away from the screen. Be intimately involved in video game purchases. Level with him as to the reasons you are instituting these rules. Consult your pediatrician if you feel the need. And if all else fails, seek professional help.

If you feel your child is becoming or has become addicted, do not just institute the above suggestions and leave it at that. You have been presented with a special challenge, to teach your child to live with computers and the video game console. Teaching self-control is difficult, but it is the most important tool you can provide a child prone to any addiction.

Cell Phones

By the time your preteen becomes a teen, he or she will own a cell phone. At least, nearly nine out of ten of them will. Nearly as many will own an iPod or other MP3 player as well.

How about preteens? According to one Zogby study, about one-third of preteens owns a cell phone. You may not realize it, but companies are much more ahead of the game than you, and they have for some time now developed cell phones *specifically* for this age group. Have you ever purchased a cute little toy from LeapFrog for your preschooler? Now, such companies also provide cell phones for kids. These phones often lack a traditional keypad, and provide instructions to parents who can program in the numbers that can be "dialed" from the phone's limited keypad buttons. Many come with educational games as well and offer basic text messaging to and from parents.

Of course, many preteens, and especially teenagers, will want a "real" phone. And there are again many choices, from typical "adult" phones to phones by Disney and more. There are two basic choices to be made with these types of phones. The first is whether to get a pre-paid plan or a family plan. The pre-paid plan has the advantage of (perhaps) teaching your children some responsibility, as when the minutes are up, well, the minutes are up. Then again, the last thing you want is for your kids to use up their minutes just prior to some emergency where they need to get in touch with you. An alternative is to put them on your family plan and teach responsibility using other methods.

A second choice is whether to purchase a phone with tracking technology. Phones today can come with GPS or other tracking systems. By punching in a password on a website, you can instantly find out where your kids are. Is this a great tool for keeping kids safe, or is it a terribly insidious way for parents to spy on their kids? I do not think there is any "right" choice to be made here. Consider a child who lives in an urban center and takes a train, and then has to walk several city blocks, to get to school. You can imagine such a kid *wanting* his phone to have GPS capabilities so his parents know, if something terrible occurs, where he is. Now think of a typical suburban kid who just cannot stand the fact that his parents are "looking over his shoulder" with this new spying technology. You can imagine such a kid leaving his phone in a "safe" location or turning it off entirely just to spite his parents. Then what happens when there is an emergency?

In the end, it is a difficult decision to make. Ultimately it has to be a choice the parents are comfortable with, and probably the kids as well. Some parents make a pact with their children, promising to never track them unless there is an emergency. Whatever your situation, talking to your children about the reasons why you might want to track is important. On the other hand, allowing them to have a phone that does not track could be used to show your trust in them. Of course, let them know that if that trust is ever violated, their next phone will be a GPS phone.

Media Literacy and Advertising

Since we last spoke about ads—in the preschool years—your children have in all likelihood attained a much more nuanced understanding of advertising. Up until now, kids have tended to view ads as just another form of entertainment, or at the very least, they do not yet understand that the information from commercials can be biased.

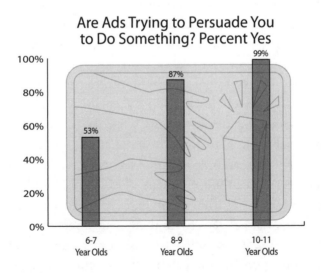

Are Ads Trying to Persuade You to Do Something? Percent Yes

Source: Bergler

But the next, and crucial step in understanding advertising is to realize that in the attempt to persuade, ads may contain bias and deception.

Percent Who Think Ads Only Sometimes or Never Tell the Truth

Source: Bergler

The good news is that as children come to understand the persuasive—and deceptively persuasive—nature of advertising, their liking of advertisements precipitously drops. And as children move through their preteen years they gain a much better understanding of not just the overarching goals of ads but how each specific element plays its own role, from the music selected to the number of times they show the name of the product. The problem still remains, however (and will for a long time) that children as old as their preteen years are at risk because they are being exposed to ads, but have little ability to view ads critically.

So what is the big deal about advertising? First there is the concern that advertising gets an unfair advantage since your children start seeing ads long before they understand they have a persuasive intent, and second, that the persuasion embedded in them often involves bias and deception.

Certainly, parents agree that advertising to children is unfair. A majority of Americans feel that there should be limits on junk food advertising to children, and nearly four out of five adults feel there should be limits on advertising to children in general.

There is not much a parent can do about ads, at least at first. If a child is not cognitively developed enough to understand the nuances of persuasion, then there is little that can be done except to wait. When your children get to a point where they understand such concepts, then you can begin to inoculate, even though now you can only inoculate your child against future viewing, not, of course, what they have already seen.

The second concern with advertising is the socialization of children toward materialism. We train our kids, it is argued, to want to buy, to want to own, and to want a lot of it. You don't need scientists to prove to you that kids begin to favor and horde their toys as valuable possessions as early as two years of age (my kids must own 20 little wooden toy trains, so why does it seem like they are always fighting over the same one?). Advertisements can make this wanting all the more powerful and intense. In one experiment, researchers showed one group of children ages four and five an advertisement for a new toy, but did not show the ad to another group. They then gave each child a choice to play with one of two playmates: one who happened to own that same advertised toy and one that did not. While a third of the children who did not see the ad chose the playmate with the toy, twice as many who saw the ad chose the toy-laden playmate, no doubt planning to get their hands on that toy!

It is certainly the case that, as we get older, we develop more sophisticated reasons for owning things. While first graders tend to just want more and more, preteens more often want to own things to help develop their personality. Owning unique things, preteens think, makes you unique as a person.

But the point to remember here is that, yes, developing a materialistic sense is probably inevitable, and in many ways, not such a bad thing (humans need motivation, after all. If wanting a car means your high schooler will work nights while still staying on the honor role, that is not necessarily an evil, materialistic thing). The more one watches television, the more one wants things. But in case that does not concern you much, try this one out: The more they want to own, the more you, as a parent, have to say no. And researchers have consistently found that the more materialistic your children are, the more arguments you are going to have over purchases.

One of the more concerning areas of advertising for many health researchers is food advertising. Food advertising starts early: From age two through seven, children see about twelve food ads a day. That number goes up to twenty-one ads per day by the preteen years. Children see more ads for food than for any other type of product. Nearly four out of every five of these ads are for candy, cereal, or fast food. And conversely, preteens are only likely to see an advertisement that promotes fitness of any kind about twice a week. So it is important to make your kids aware of the prevalence of food ads and to understand how they gravitate toward candy and fast food.

What You Can Do About Advertising

First, you could do nothing. Your children are going to be exposed to advertisements. How many is a number in that varies from one researcher to another, but they all agree, it is a lot. Some researchers argue that a typical teenager can be exposed to thousands of ads per day via billboards, Internet banners, television, etc. And really, there is nothing you can do about it.

But the second answer is, train your child to be media literate. In a word, inoculate. Becoming media literate means learning to think about media as you watch it, rather than acting like some automaton couch potato whose only purpose is to be entertained. Most parents I know get intimidated by the thought of learning and teaching media literacy. But here is the thing: you are already halfway there. There is no need to feel intimidated because you are already teaching media literacy to your child.

It is important to show your children, then, exactly why advertisements and shows are designed the way they are. Pick any one advertisement targeting a preteen and you will find, in all likelihood, that everything about that commercial, from the music in the background, to the actors, how they are dressed, what they say, and how they say it, the color scheme, the camera angles, etc., all are designed at identification. If you, the viewer, in any way identify with that ad, you are halfway to being sold on the product.

We are now moving away from a model of parent-as-armor, that is teaching parents how to shield and protect their children from the potentially harmful effects of the mass media, to a model of giving kids armor of their own, since increasingly, the media choices they make move out of your control. Your kids are no doubt starting to really get out there, meaning out from under your protective wing. Many now have media sources in their own room, from television to the Internet, though I advise against either setup: Until you become an empty nester, you should keep these media in a public place. But regardless, there is school, and friends' houses, and you have little control over what they are exposed to there. And even in your own home, your children will increasingly exert their independence and watch programs designed for adults.

That inevitability means violent programming, slicker advertising, and mature subject matter. So now is the time. Talk to your kids about media. Plan for more than one talk. Give them the skills to protect themselves, and let them know what good decision making is all about when it comes to growing up with mass media.

CHAPTER 5 CHEAT SHEET

TELEVISION

KEY CONCERN	Wanting to be thin but possibly getting fatter, plus other messages from television.
REMEDY	Inoculate preteens from messages and images.

COMPUTERS AND INTERNET

KEY CONCERNS	Predators and bullying.
REMEDY	Learn what is necessary to help your kids avoid these concerns.

VIDEO GAMES

KEY CONCERN	Overuse and violence.
REMEDY	Choose games wisely, moderate and mediate use.

ADVERTISING AND MEDIA LITERACY

KEY CONCERNS	Advertising influence.
REMEDY	Begin media literacy.

6

Middle School

IF THERE IS ONE WORD that comes to mind, I think, when one thinks of the middle school experience, it is this: hormones. This is the time of boys to men, girls to women. For guys, it's all about finding that first hint of facial hair and trying to not get embarrassed by that cracking voice. And of course, the girls have more serious changes occurring. A few generations ago, the thought that one's first boyfriend or girlfriend would pop up in the 6th, 7th, or even 8th grade was shocking. Now, it's normal, and has been for some time. Students often get their first real (that is, not just puppy love) infatuation with a teacher or some other adult at this age. So let's stop beating around the bush, shall we? These are the years when sex is on the brain: What it is, how it feels and oh, I can't stop thinking about it thanks to the hormones I never knew I had.

So at this point it should not surprise you that the main topic of this chapter is the media and sex. We are increasingly realizing that we are dealing with (very) young men and women, not boys and girls anymore. I know, as a parent we are probably years from giving up the thought that our kids are our little children, but from the standpoint of your children, they are ready and willing to act like adults. In fact, the changes happening in their bodies often validate to them that they are in fact, adults.

Television and Movies

If there is one thing certain about television, it is that skin sells. Close your eyes and tell me what pops into your heads when you think about the following: Beer commercials. *Baywatch*. Hanes commercials. *Survivor*. Music videos. And yes, even the wholesome goodness of *Dancing with the Stars*. The answer I think is pretty obvious: skin sells. Studies of television have found that there about two instances of intimate touching in the average one hour of primetime television. Kissing occurs nearly just as much. Over the decades, portrayals of sexual intercourse have increased steadily through the years. This focus on sex, sexy images, sexual dialogue, and sexual innuendo does have some important effects on our pubescent teenagers. After all, to them, this is all new. To them it truly is eye candy.

Sex and the Mass Media

There are generally three areas with which researchers are concerned when it comes to sex and the mass media. Like many other areas of study on the mass media, there is first the question of knowledge and opinion. In this case, we are talking about the degree to which people think the sexual content they watch and how it's discussed and dealt with on TV is real. Second is media's impact on our attitudes about sex (such as whether we think certain sexual behavior is okay). Finally, of course, there is the question as to whether sex in the media actually affects one's own sexual activity.

It should certainly come as no surprise that the more one consumes media, the more one is likely to feel that the portrayals of sex and relationships in the media are real. And this is key because if one finds it to be real, than one has no reason whatsoever to not mimic such behavior.

Okay, but is the media really filled with sex? The answer is, absolutely. In one study by Sapolsky and Tabarlet, media were divided into small elements and each element was labeled as having no sexual content or some sexual content. If there was sexual content, the researchers further classified each element as containing one or many of a number of possible types of content, from touching and kissing to discussion about relationships to sexual intercourse. For example, the 20 most popular movies in 2004 were sliced into segments, defined by any break of sequence or camera cut, which occurred, on average, every 6.4 seconds. Similar slicing was done by Pardun, L'Engle and Brown for the most popular television shows, music videos, magazines, newspapers, and Internet sites. So how much of each type of media contains sexual content?

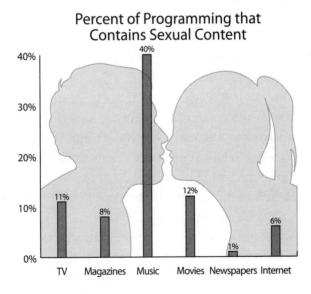

Percent of Programming that Contains Sexual Content

Source: Pardun, L'Engle and Brown

As you can see from the chart on the previous page, music videos are the clear winner, with two out of every five scenes containing sexual content. For television and movies, its one out of ten elements or scenes. Of course, print media contains much less sexual content.

While these numbers might not be shocking, it is important to keep in mind a few caveats. First, segments were defined as having either some form of nudity (partial or full), relational issues, sexual innuendo, touching and kissing, intercourse, or general pubertal issues. By a long shot, the most prominent form of sex in media is nudity:

Sexual Content in the Media	
Nudity	41%
Relationships	25%
Sexual Innuendo	12%
Touching/Kissing	14%
Intercourse	7%

Source: Pardun, L'Engle and Brown

The second thing to consider is that most kids consume a vast amount of media. Thus the fact that "only" eleven percent of television is sexual means that for most kids, they are consuming hours of sexual content each week. Finally, one should remember that every kid is different. If one were to primarily watch national news and documentary-type shows, for example, one would not be nearly as exposed as someone who watched a lot of R-rated movies and late prime time (9 P.M. or later) programming. So there is of course a wide range here, with some kids watching television that contains less than 5 percent sexual content, and others that may be as high as 50 percent.

Does Heavy Consumption of Sex in the Media Affect Teenagers Negatively?

There has been some mixed evidence, but by far, the lion's share of studies find that indeed, sexual content in the media influences people's knowledge, attitudes, and beliefs about sex. For one, the more you watch, the more you think that everybody is having sex; or at least, a lot more often than they really are. And, since the television shows so many instances of extramarital affairs, sex without love, sex being used for favors (such as in the work environment), and sex as a form of conquest, most people who watch a lot of television, and consume other media as well, inflate the frequency with which extramarital affairs, sex without love, etc., occur in the real world.

And watching does not just convince us that there is a lot of "bad" (again, extramarital, without love, with aggression, etc.) sex out there. It also convinces us that bad sex is okay. Both surveys and experimental research have consistently shown that watching television with sexual content leads to more permissive attitudes toward marital infidelity and other sexual transgressions. Given the degree to which music videos contain sexual content, it should be of no surprise that this type of media has some of the strongest effects of all, and that specifically those who watch a lot of music videos tend to also have some of the highest average measures of acceptance of premarital sex amongst all teenagers.

It is important to note, then, that teenagers seem to follow the media's message about sex, whatever that message may be. So if media show an extramarital affair leading to a broken home, lots of anguish, and other negative outcomes for the transgressor, then the watcher is more likely to consider extramarital sex a bad thing. But the media does not seem to exhibit such instances nearly as much as they do instances where there is little or no punishment for this kind of immoral behavior.

Attitudes are one thing, but behavior is another thing entirely. So let's cut to the chase: The initiation of sex. Surely, you say, sex in the media doesn't affect when my child is going to make the decision to first have sex with another? Unfortunately, it very much looks like it does.

How the Media Affects Kids' Choices Regarding Sex

One study by Collins and colleagues measured the top twenty-three programs watched by teenagers, and then measured these shows for sexual content. From this they were able to measure how much sexual content each person consumed on television. The study looked at teenagers ages twelve to seventeen. Researchers recontacted these teenagers a year later to see if they had initiated sex during the past year. What they found was that eight percent of fourteen-year-olds who watched very little sexual media initiated sex in that year. However, among fourteen-year-olds who consumed a lot of sexual content, the number was nearly double. Similarly, twenty-four percent of seventeen-year-olds who consumed very low levels of sexual television initiated sex, compared to thirty-six percent of high sexual content consuming teenagers.

But teenagers don't just initiate sex. As we all remember from our school days, sex is like baseball: You have to get to first base, then second, then third, before you hit a home run. Take the average fifteen-year-old, for instance. Twenty percent of fifteen-year-olds who watched very little sexual content initiated genital touching (third base) in the following year. But for high sexual content fifteen-year-olds, that number was forty-two percent, a substantial increase.

Unfortunately, you never know if there is some other reason for these differences lurking in the background. However, these types of studies do attempt to think through what these differences might be, and attempt to control them mathematically in their research. Even with these controls, they are finding these effects. True, it still may be the case that they have not found and controlled for everything they should, and it may be the case that general sexual interests or libido could drive *both* the watching of sexual television and the initiation of sex. But given all we know about the effects of mass media, and the care with which these researchers tend to design their studies, it would be surprising if media did not have some effect on our teenager's perceptions of sex, their attitudes toward sex, and even their behavior.

The Darker Side of Sex on TV and in Movies

So certainly, sexual content in the media can negatively (or prohibitively) influence your children's attitudes and behaviors about sex and relationships. Unfortunately, there are other potential effects of sex in the mass media that could be of much greater concern. These include the viewing of extreme sex, rather than the usual heavy petting that goes along with your typical PG-13 movie. What about exposure to sexual degradation of women? What about when violence and sex intermingle, such as with rape scenes in movies and television shows? And finally, what about pornography?

In one study, researchers split people into four main groups. One watched a number of hours of violent R-rated "slasher" movies. These movies contained violence toward women, as well as erotic sex scenes. A second group watched the same amount of X-rated, though nonviolent, pornographic movies, and a third group watched R-rated movies that contained no violence and only what is regarded as basic "teen sex." A final group watched nothing for comparison. Later, these same subjects answered a questionnaire and watched a reenacted sexual assault trial, for which they judged the defendant and answered questions regarding the trial.

The only group that showed significant differences was the violent/sexual R-rated "slasher" film group. People in this group were found to be much less sympathetic to the victim in the trial and toward rape victims in general. For example, their judgment of how much the woman was injured during the alleged assault was lower for those who watched violent R-rated moves than for those that did not. They also found people who watch R-rated violent slasher films, like the rest of us, were initially disturbed when viewing such content. Unfortunately, as you might expect, the researchers found that the more people watched such movies, the less these movies produced anxious and depressive thoughts. Indeed, other research finds that the content in these movies is actually interpreted over time as less violent and less degrading to women, and, that over time, more people report enjoying these movies.

Studying Pornography

What about X-rated, but nonviolent movies? Watching nonviolent pornography has been shown to influence attitudes, if only in the short term. But what about over the longer term? Does pornography impact people beyond just directly after they get experimented on? The problem is that pornography research is limited because it is hard to get people to willingly expose themselves to pornography over a long period of time, and indeed, it is arguably unethical to ask ordinary, non-pornography-watching people to suddenly watch pornography on a daily basis for weeks at a time.

So mostly, researchers have focused on short and medium exposure effects. Short exposure equals a change in attitudes that lasts hours or perhaps days. Medium term is relatively longer, but still, an attitude that will likely go away after not watching pornography for a small amount of time.

First, pornography makes one more tolerant of more bizarre forms of sexual activity. As I have said before, probably not the effect you wish upon your young adults. As for the degradation of women, there is evidence that pornography does, like violence, affect attitudes regarding the victim in mock rape trials. Here, researchers found that persons who viewed pornography gave a lighter punishment to the offender than those who did not watch pornography. The researchers also found that viewers of porn were less likely to agree with statements in support of sexual equality between the sexes.

Behavior and Pornography

Finally, there is the disheartening question of behavior and pornography: Does pornography lead to an elevated chance one might become sexually aggressive, even to the extreme of rape? The good news is, from a correlational perspective, the answer seems to be no, according to Bauserman's review of the research: Sexual offenders do not report using pornography in their teenage years, and even adult years, any more than nonoffenders. Indeed, in a handful of studies, the nonoffenders used pornography *more* than the offenders. This is good news indeed, as it says that finding your middle schooler with sexually explicit magazines or DVDs does *not* mean he is a future convict. In fact, in many of these studies, the nonoffenders were also found to possess pornography at earlier ages than the offenders!

Furthermore, rapes do not always occur more in places where there is a larger circulation of pornography. True, some studies have found a moderate link; however, upon further examination researchers suspect there is something else going on. Similar to other research of sexual content mentioned earlier, there is likely some other attribute in people that is associated with BOTH pornography and sexual violence. One hint of trouble comes from a study that found, oddly enough, a higher viewership of *Playgirl* is associated with a larger number of rapes. Unfortunately, since *Playgirl* has a largely women-based readership, it is hard to imagine that effect is real, unless is it just a sign that something else is going on other than a direct link between overall pornography circulation and sexual crimes. To this day, researchers continue to explore the issue, and are not at all confident that the availability of pornography has any impact at all on the likelihood of someone committing a sex crime.

Other data find that the rate of rapes increase as use of pornography increases. In the 1960s, for example, the pornography consumption increased some 700 percent. However, there was no difference in the crime rate for violent sexual offenses; rather, the rate of rape and other violent sexually crimes perfectly followed the overall crime rate year by year. Similarly, rape does not occur more in areas with a greater frequency of adult movie theaters.

One of the more recent studies, however, did find an effect, between past pornography use and being found guilty of a violent crime. Researchers have found that exposure to pornography was generally related to sexual aggression, hostility toward women, acceptance of rape myths, and sexual dominance. However, follow-up studies discovered that when they separated out the few people in the study who were *extremely* high consumers of pornography, the remaining respondents were completely normal with regard to sexual hostility, acceptance of rape myth, and all the other measures. However, those who consumed a lot of pornography also scored extremely high on potential aggression toward women and most other measures. The point is, the study did not find any greater likelihood of becoming a sex offender among people who watched some or even a moderate amount of pornography. It was only those who consumed a very high amount of pornography that exhibited potential warning signs of sexual aggression.

So What's To Be Done About Sex in the Media?

Not to shock you about something you might not know, but the viewing of explicit sexual material by teenagers is largely done in private (gasp!). On the other hand, with the prevalence of sex in the media today, your kids probably watch a lot a material with sexual undertones (and overtones) right in front of your eyes, and you don't give it a second thought. Thus, there is one strategy for everyday sexual content, and another for explicit content. You might expect me to say that with regard to sexual content, you should be using some of the same approaches I've suggested elsewhere in this book: co-viewing and explanation.

The real question is, how? Researchers have explored different communication strategies regarding how to talk to your kids about sex in the media. However, some have been found to cause as much harm as good.

There are a number of communicative strategies a parent can take in approaching a frank discussion about sexual media with their children. One strategy is called "negative mediation," when parents criticize media while allowing kids to still watch. A second type is called "positive mediation," which is when parents praise shows or other media. Of course this is something you probably don't want to do toward media with sexual content! Then of course, "neutral mediation" is when parents discuss media but are noncommittal about it. A fourth type is called "restrictive mediation," which is when parents refuse to allow their children to watch specific shows, and when it is allowed, restrict how long their kids can watch. Another form of mediation is "interactive mediation," which is essentially using media to open up a dialogue about that media. The dialogue is meant to be interactive, where opinions of many kinds are heard. Finally, there is "co-viewing," which is a "watch but don't talk" policy.

We have reviewed this to some extent already, as there is much to be said about watching educational television with your toddler, pre-schooler, and early elementary school children. Co-viewing alone was found to have positive effects. Interactive viewing of any kind also increased learning. But what about now that your child is a young adult? And now that the media is not educational television but television (movies, etc.) that contains sexual content?

The problem is that teenagers are, well, you know, teenagers. Have you perhaps tried restrictive mediation on your teenager yet? Chances are, you were not well-received. Not that being well-received is a necessary aspect of the parent-teenager relationship! But in the end, you want it to sink in. The fear is that restrictive mediation may backfire. Studies in fact show that parents with an authoritarian personality run the risk of having it backfire in general, leading to children more apt to be more delinquent in some fashion. Indeed, studies have even found that sexual promiscuity among teenagers is more likely among teenagers whose parents are either highly authoritative or not at all authoritative.

What Can You Do About Sex in Movies and Television?

The best plan of action, research strongly suggests, is the middle road, the carrot and stick. In short, parents need to communicate, and realize that control only goes so far anymore. Being able to talk about sex and other topics is hugely beneficial for kids. Parents who broach the topic comfortably tend to be closer to their children, and their children, on average, make better decisions.

And here you go, how do you break the ice? How do you give the birds and bees speech, and keep the dialogue going? One possibility is, to use the media as the ice breaker. Mediate interactively with your kids. When sexual content is shown, talk about it. Make a joke about it to start the conversation. Or wait until the show is over. You will probably find this much easier than starting up a conversation from scratch.

Indeed, research finds that the "middle road" is the most effective. How do kids react to parents that restrict content? You may think they react by seeking out that content even more than before, to even become infatuated with it. And you would be right, as this is exactly what scientific research

Ways to Watch Media with Your Child

Here are six methods a parent can use when interacting with the children and the mass media:

1. **Negative Mediation:** Voicing critical opinions of something that is watched.
2. **Positive Mediation:** Voicing positive opinions about media.
3. **Neutral Mediation:** Noncommittal talking about media.
4. **Restrictive Mediation:** Prohibiting kids from consuming certain media, or allowing them the media but limiting the amount of exposure.
5. **Interactive Mediation:** Conversations about media that can contain positive, negative, and neutral messages.
6. **Co-Viewing:** Watching, listening, or otherwise interacting with media with your children, without any verbal commentary.

has shown. Kids who have restrictive parents also, on average, rate them less favorably than nonrestrictive parents (no surprise). Finally, kids of restrictive parents report viewing media their parents would find offensive more frequently with their friends (presumably at their friend's houses) than kids of less restrictive parents.

On the other hand, it does not pay to just sit and watch. Most research suggests that co-viewing of sexual material is akin to your giving tacit agreement to such behaviors. In one study, basic co-viewing of media with sexual content was found to increase favorable attitudes toward teenage sex.

The best path toward success is nonrestrictive mediation of some kind. This can be a hard pill to swallow for many parents. Indeed, most parents who practice restrictive mediation are those who personally find sexual content the most offensive. It is hard to allow exposure to media that you yourself find distasteful. If you cannot openly allow for such exposure, at the least, try negative mediation. Sure, most studies find negative mediation to be distasteful to teens (who tend to be sensitive to being "lectured" by mom and dad). But few have found negative consequences beyond the "lecture effect."

While this method is often the most difficult, you need to be up for the challenge. You are taking the first positive steps by reading this book. Interactive mediation means to have probing conversations with your children. A columnist I recently read said that, of all places, *Mad Magazine* once told him the best advice on dealing with teenagers: In short, if you want to avoid them acting like children, treat them like adults. But while treating them like adults, challenge the media they are watching, without challenging *them*. Talk about what you know in terms of the effect such programming can have on people. Talk about how media are far more sexed up than real life. In the media, people do more extravagant things, more often, and unfortunately, often with far less passion than one might feel in real life. And that is an important message, that while mediated sex might be more bountiful, it can never replicate how intimate and special a connection with a loved one can be. Talk about the differences between the morals people tend to exhibit on television and your family's morals, your friend's parent's morals, and the morals of society in general. But do it in a conversation. Let them speak as much as you speak yourself.

Smoking in Television and Movies

As long as we have had motion pictures, actors and actresses have smoked. While smoking has become less of an issue, all it takes is for your teenager to think one smoker on the screen is cool. The "good" news is that more people smoke in real life than on television. The bad news is that about twice as many characters smoke in the movies than do in real life. And, most depictions of smokers in the movies tend to cast them in a neutral or even positive light. There are few examples of characters who smoke and hate themselves for it. And of course, in print media, the concern is not the actors but the commercials, which of course are going to associate smoking with other cool things.

Like all other effects of the mass media, the potential impact of the mass media on smoking begins with whether the media changes our opinions of how many people smoke. In a basic study by Page conducted about ten years ago, college students guessed that about twice as many people smoke as were actual smokers. However, the study did not make an explicit link to watching a lot of movies, which is presumably the only place one might gain an inflated sense of who smokes. Indeed, if one were to only watch television, one might actually underestimate the number of smokers.

While there is uncertainty whether the mass media influences how much we think we smoke, there is certainly evidence, like that by Dalton and colleagues, that heavy movie viewers are much more likely to hold positive attitudes about smoking and even initiate smoking.

The good news about attitudes toward smoking is that as much as movies can increase adolescent's positive attitudes toward smoking, anti-smoking commercials are just as effective at enacting a negative attitude toward smoking. But what really motivates teenagers is what their idols are saying and doing. And a number of studies show that movie stars in particular can have a strong influence on experimentation with smoking and attitudes toward smoking.

The main concern is with the actual initiation of smoking among young people. Here, the evidence is quite clear that heavy movie watching can and does influence a teenager's decision to start smoking. Specifically, a study of over 3,500 adolescents measured the number of movies they watched. A follow-up study then measured whether they had initiated smoking one to two years later. While ten percent started to smoke overall, seventeen percent of the top twenty-five percent of movie watchers started to smoke. In fact, shown on a graph (see facing page), the results were quite strikingThese effects were even worse if one's parents smoked. But overall, clearly, there appears to be some impact of the glamorization of smoking and the initiation of smoking among adolescents. The good news is that anti-smoking messages appear to be as effective as smoking messages. The first place to start is to quit yourself, and preferably, before they are teens. If you smoke you will find it very difficult to effectively persuade your kids to not smoke.

Second, talk to your kids about smoking. There are many effective strategies for doing so, and I encourage you to go

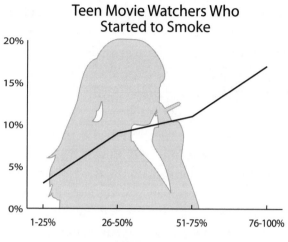

Teen Movie Watchers Who Started to Smoke

20%

15%

10%

5%

0%

| 1-25% | 26-50% | 51-75% | 76-100% |

Percent of Kids Who Watch Fewer
Movies Than the Teen Answering the Survey

Source: Dalton, Sargent, Beach et al.

to any number of websites dedicated to this subject, such as *www.thetruth.com* and *www.anti-smoking.org.* Finally, talk to your kids about Hollywood smoking. Let them know that in real life, few of the actors they see in the movies smoke. Explain to them that in past generations, smoking was popular in part because people had very little idea of its long term harmful effects on one's health. Thus, movies set in the past will contain a lot of smoking, but that does not mean it is acceptable to smoke in the present day.

Computers and the Internet

By now, your teenager will almost certainly have had quite a bit of practice using the Internet, cell phones, instant messaging, even chatting. So what do they do with all these skills?

They use them in real life. If there is one indubitable difference between myself and my kids, it will be that my use of the Internet will be for consumer research; for your teens it will be for that *and* for personal communication *and* for personality projection. Cell phones for you are for communication, just like the good old landline on your parent's kitchen wall. For your teen, they will also use it as their version of the notes you once passed from one student to another in class. They will use it to check news, scores, and even their web spaces. Maybe you use instant messages regularly, maybe not. Your teen will use it like any other form of communication, and possibly, use it a lot. I have to admit, other than for classroom purposes and research for this book, my only chat room exposure is belonging to an online forum on digital astrophotography! Not quite what your kid has in mind when he goes to chat.

Perhaps it would be wise to note what you might expect from your teenager and all these new forms of communication. What you might find is that *The Matrix* lives. That's right, the great Keanu Reeves movie, and its two horrible sequels. In that movie, people lived in two worlds, the real and the virtual. Guess what? Your kids live in both worlds as well. But it is important to understand that both worlds are irrevocably linked.

The method of communication (real or electronic) can affect *how* we see someone, though at the core, they are the same person. So just as Neo's virtual character was more clean cut and cooler than his disheveled real personality, so too your kids are showing people only what they want to show them online. Indeed, some online personalities resemble nothing like the person behind them. It all starts by first reaching out online, and that is where we begin.

Developing an Electronic Social Network

According to the Pew Internet and American Life Project, well over half of all teenagers have an online profile. So chances are good your teen is out there. Only two thirds presently claim to be able to limit access to their profiles. Half of those with an online profile admit to lying about themselves online. Again, about half say they use their online profile to make new friends. And over a third have been contacted by an online stranger.

What are online profiles, anyway? According to the Pew and Internet Life Project, teens with an online profile have the following information about themselves out there:

Teens with Online Profiles: What Information Do They Post?	
First Name	82%
Photo of Self	79%
Photo of Friends	66%
Name of Hometown	61%
Name of School	49%
Instant Message Name	40%
Last Name	29%
E-mail Address	29%

Source: Pew Internet and American Life Project

Being online is a way of life for most teens. Indeed, the percent of teens who say they are online everyday is up 50 percent, to nearly one-third and all teenagers. Nine out of ten use the Internet, which means that over half of all teenagers go online every day.

Importantly, one out of every four parents is unaware that their child has an online presence. Certainly, these also happen to be parents who are generally clueless about the Internet and its vast array of communication opportunities, and by this point in the book, that is almost certainly not you.

It probably makes sense that it is possible to have a significant percent of your daily communication move electronically, even though that is possibly not the case for you. How does this happen, exactly?

Social Networking Sites

The typical online profiling site, like MySpace or Facebook, contains multiple options for communicating with others. The first step is often to link up with your friends. This is as simple as text messaging their online profile name so they can be invited to be part of a network of friends. Then, friends can communicate a few different ways. They can post a message to their friend's profile (or wall). They can post comments on their friend's blog (to be discussed shortly). Shorter notes of encouragement and the like can be sent as "e-props" or "pokes." Messages can include graphics, from smiley icons (emoticons) to full blown photos. Finally, a more common form is to post messages to group networks, much like I would do on my astrophotography group. Teens who are connected in this way tend to make it an important aspect of their social lives. They report a strong feeling of being part of a group when they are connected to others. To them, it is a social connection as real as hanging out at the mall. And it is.

Simply put, teens use online social networking to make friends and to foster those relationships. One might ask, are these friends just down the street or 500 miles away? The answer is, either. Or both. One example is a teen who was part of a recent Pew study, who noted that his high school was too big for him to effectively track down and meet people. But online, you can look at people's online profiles, see what they are into, and then send someone a post or message. After a bit of back and forth, you set up a meeting in person at school. In a way, it really isn't a bad way to meet new friends.

It is important to remember that, despite real concerns about cyber bullying many teens feel that it is less appropriate to be rude or demeaning online than in person. So from another perspective, it can certainly be the case that making friends online feels safer than in person.

In addition to meeting friends, online communication strengthens preexisting relationships. About half of teens feel this way about their online presence. Furthermore, teens do not feel their time online takes away from real face time, but is rather in addition to the time they spend face-to-face.

Of course there are concerns about meeting strangers, again, something I have discussed in earlier chapters. Certainly, these fears are real, but overall, only one in five teenagers who are online report having a substantial friend online that they have never met in person. And of course, most of these are harmless; pen pals, friends of friends, and people who have reached out (or been taken in) because of a common interest in a hobby or activity.

From the point of view of your teenager, their online presence could be a more accurate representation of who they are. There is first of all the dissociation with looks, in that online, you don't have to show your face (and body). Thus, the online personality is less bound to this all-too-important aspect of face-to-face communication.

Yet despite feeling their online self is more "true" than their true self, they also admit to having more than one personality online (so which is most accurate, one has to ask?). As much as one quarter of teens with an online profile, in fact, have four or more different e-mail addresses or screen names. One screen name is most likely used for only their closest friends, perhaps two to seven people. Then there are other groups connected to other friends and their friends. But on the other hand, teens also use their different profiles to sometimes "try out" different aspects of their online personality. This is no different than you or I did when we were their age: we just had to do it in person.

Overall, though, there is no reason to think your teen's online life is anything but normal, unless you witness or are told of cyber bullying, or you feel your teen is simply spending too much of his time communicating online.

In addition to online profiles and communities, your teen is likely also communicating through the use of an instant messenger. Currently, about three out of every four teens who go online use instant messaging, and a third of these say they use it everyday. About half of all teens who go online check or send an instant message every time they go online.

Blogs and Webpages

Teens are also blogging. Blogs are today's journals and diaries. However, because they are on the Internet, usually as part of one's own web space or online community profile, they are public. On the other hand, never has a generation become so active in written communication as today's generation. Blogs don't hurt in terms of reading either, as teens don't just write their own, they read others as well. About one teen out of five blogs. They keep blogs for a number of reasons. Many use it as a parent-free zone to vent and discuss topics with friends that aren't easily accommodated by "fast" forms of communication like instant messaging. Blogs teach teens to have their own voice. It's not just about getting yourself out there; it is about exploring yourself and learning as you go.

Your teen may also have his or her own webpage. About a third of teens who go online have created webpages for themselves or others, or at least have created blogs for themselves of others. About a quarter actually develops and maintains their own webpages.

Cell Phones

Finally, your teen is probably connected to the cell phone (perhaps you think it is glued to their heads sometimes!). About half of teens presently own cell phones. This number is much higher amongst average-to higher-than-average-income families. About one third of teenagers use cell phone text messages as a form of communication as well. This is not to say that teens eschew the old landline phone. Over half of all conversations with friends still occur using a regular phone.

But overall, it is important to note, as did the Pew Internet and American Life Project, that teens that seem inordinately "wired" still have full and productive offline lives. Four out of five participate in some sort of after school activity. Most have a strong group of friends they interact with, above all else, in person. But it is, nevertheless, still the case that teens now have two very significant avenues in which to be a teen, the offline and the online.

Internet Pornography

The Internet has once been described as being "pornography on steroids." While this is most certainly exaggerating the problem, there is no question that the Internet has been as much of a boon for pornographers as for just about any other industry. Take spam e-mails, for instance. Most people think of spam as the Internet's version of the telemarketing call. But it is very different, since around twenty percent of spam contains adult content. Nearly half of all teenagers, it is estimated, currently receive pornography spam every single day.

The number of Internet sites dedicated to pornography is now practically uncountable. Estimates put the number at somewhere over a half a billion web pages, and half a million websites. It is estimated that nearly 100 million people world-wide visit an adult site each week.

When we discussed pornography on screen media, the problem was centered around teenagers seeking out such content. The same is true for the Internet, but addition-ally, there is the concern over inadvertent exposure. At least twenty-five percent of all teenagers are exposed to unwanted sexually explicit material each year according to research by Greenfield. Two out of five were exposed not just to pictures of naked people but to pictures of intercourse, and one in ten were actually exposed to violent sexual content. About three quarters have viewed pornography inadvertently while browsing the Internet, while the other quarter will open up an e-mail that unexpectedly contains sexual content.

Surely, teens don't just stumble upon pornography. Many seek it out. There is uncertainty as to how many teens seek out Internet pornography, but some estimates are as high as fifteen percent. At least fifteen percent of teenagers have admitted in surveys to lying about their ages to gain access to a website, though not all websites that ask for one's age (or to certify that their age is at least 18) contain explicit sexual content. Looking at the issue another way, what percent of visitors to porno-graphic sites are underage? Again, the numbers vary, but most estimates fall within the fifteen to twenty-five percent range. Regardless of how many do go to pornographic sites, a major-ity of teens say that they can visit a pornographic site without their parents ever knowing it. And they are probably right.

One substantial impact the Internet has had on society is to drastically increase the amount of material one can access on very specialized subjects. That is to say, not only has the Internet increased the availability of information regarding the most general of subjects, like pornography, but it has even more so increased the availability of specialized interests, such as specific subsets of pornography. This includes all sorts of fetishes such as latex wear, domination, and submission, but also many of the darkest corners of the world of pornography, such as asphyxiation, torture, and child pornography.

How to Detect a Problem with Internet Pornography

It is not always easy to figure out whether your child is consuming unsavory content on the Internet. And then, it can be even more difficult to figure out what to do about it.

The only option you have with regard to figuring out whether your child is consuming unwanted content is through your filtering software. As we have discussed, this software can tell you where your child has been, when, and for how long. Even then, it can be difficult. Often, you really have no way of knowing what that is, unless you go there

---

Napster Goes Porn

Remember the early days of music sharing, when Napster was all the rage? Within a year, millions of people were using Napster to download music for free. Nowadays, that is a dangerous proposition, as the Recording Industry Association of America has been suing heavy downloaders and distributors of music via what are now called peer-to-peer networks.

These networks, which Napster popularized, now come in all shapes and sizes like Limewire and Kaaza. To this day many people, especially teens, use these networks to download their favorite music and videos for free. Unfortunately, it is estimated that over half of the files available on these networks are no longer music files. They are sexually explicit video files, often mislabeled as harmless music videos.

yourself. But again, most filtering software can also provide you screenshots you can later view. With screenshots, there will be no question as to what your kid is viewing.

Still, a number of kids claim to know how to get around their parents filtering software, according to Pew and others. After all, kids can easily crash their computer by literally unplugging it while it is on, and all the histories in most Internet browsing software and many filtering software systems will not save any information. The computer is turned back on, and there is no information there. If you notice gaps in the timeframes noted in your filtering software, this could be why. And of course, there are many other techniques. Kids can be amazingly good at figuring out their parent's access codes. And really tech-savvy kids can get access to computer code or other programs that can disable filtering software.

Most kids are not this advanced, luckily. Still, if you suspect a problem, one method of detection is to catch your child in the act. For example, if they seem to have developed a penchant for working on the computer late, you might knock on the door at one of these times. Surely that gives kids enough time to go to another website. Still, see how your kid reacts. Ask to use the computer for a second, and further see how they react. Once on the computer, hit the back button, or click the drop down menu of web addresses, to see if there is anything there. Ultimately, it is up to you to know how far you should push it, based on your child's reaction.

How to Deal with Your Child Watching Porn

So your child viewed pornography. What do you do? Most professionals strongly advise against harsh interrogations, the third-degree, or other forms of direct confrontation. After all, there is a chance, depending on the situation, that it was inadvertent exposure. Indeed, talking to your child and communicating your feelings is the best way a parent can deal with these challenges, as well as sex education at school. In short, do not be one of those parents who continually postpones the birds and bees discussion, and who talks to their kids about sex about as much as they talk to their kids about matrix algebra. Here is not the place to have a full-blown discussion on the right way to talk to your kids about sex. But there are many resources out there. Above all, do not alienate your child. Be open and let them take a cue from you: If you are comfortable talking to them about it, they will be all the more comfortable talking to you.

Beyond communication, it may be time to step up your expertise in filtering. Review your filtering software, and make sure it is doing the following:

1. Limiting not just web pages, but e-mail and chat rooms as well.
2. Monitoring the movement of files in and out of the computer via FTP (file transfer protocols) and other methods.
3. Monitoring and possibly limiting access to newsgroups, usenets, and other groups.
4. Monitoring instant messages.
5. Allowing you, the user, to modify the list of prohibited content (and you should actually take advantage of this).
6. Determining what content is inappropriate based on multiple sources such as the PICS ratings, words in URLs (web addresses), and other methods.

Cheating with the Internet

The Internet has made a wealth of information available, indeed, more than anyone living in the mid-1980s could have ever imagined. And most importantly, a wealth of information has become electronic.

This means that cutting and pasting someone else's writing into one's own paper is easier than ever. Although the extent to which kids cheat by cutting and pasting and buying papers online is not clear, it is thought that by the time your kid goes to college, they have a ten percent chance of ever cheating on an exam or paper. And in case that was not enough, some sites now don't just allow you to buy a paper on a general topic, they will actually write the paper for you from scratch. Still other sites have people available not just to write papers but all sorts of other assignments as well. Luckily, such services do come at somewhat of a premium, as papers can cost hundreds of dollars this way. So your child would probably need a pretty good weekend job to pull this off.

And just to make this story all the sadder, a number of authors and professors who have examined the work on such websites deem it to be sub par. Those hundred of dollars don't even guarantee a child a B on the assignment.

The only real method to curb cheating is with strong moral values. In addition to teaching morals like honesty and hard work, it can also help to talk about what is lost when someone cheats, specifically, the loss of knowledge. When they consider how much their writing ability will have an effect on their life (depending upon their eventual career), it becomes critical that children realize that hard work pays off.

How Kids Are Impacted

So you might ask, in sum, how does all this new electronic media impact kids? Are they better adjusted kids? Do they have greater well-being than we did, or less? At this point, it is quite uncertain. The only research on the subject has found no difference between online and offline kids. If anything, though, the net balance is positive. Think about this for a second: You can divide teens into two groups, if you will, those with little social anxiety, and those with enough to make social situations feel anywhere from uncomfortable to downright scary. For the first group, the Internet is not making much improvement on one's social connections. Rather, it is just another way to communicate with people you already know. But of those with any level of social anxiety, the Internet offers, as we have seen, the potential to more easily break the ice. And sure enough, one study did at the least find a link between social anxiety and an increased amount of instant messaging by teens.

Music

Rock and roll is music for the young (even if us oldies still like it). It captures the essence of teen angst, teen anxiety, teen emotion, and teen hopes, dreams, true feelings. Rock and roll has been with us for a long time now, and we have become pretty comfortable with its edginess. But when does it go too far? Is there a line? And where and how is that line drawn? Remember, in the 50s some would have said it was drawn when a particular side-burned rock and roller moved his hips a certain way? Today it takes Janet Jackson losing her top for Americans to become outraged.

Although I was not a parent yet, my guess is that when the Columbine Shootings happened in 1999, every parent had the same thought: could it happen at my school? And with most such stories of teen outrage and violent behavior, one question asked is, did these teens listen to heavy metal, rap, or other offensive music?

Does Offensive Music Make Violent Kids?

As you may suspect, research on the impact of this type of music has followed a typical pattern. First, researchers find a correlation between offensive music and bad behavior by conducting surveys of teens. But of course, the counter argument goes, who else is going to listen to harmful music other than teens who want to do harm? Meaning, the music has nothing to do with their bad behavior; these kids were bad seeds in the first place and the music they listen to just follows suit.

Researchers started to look at experimental settings, where they can expose people to either nonoffensive or offensive music and see if the people who listened to offensive music then did offensive things or had illicit thoughts. Johnson and colleagues, Hansen and Hansen, and others, find that, yes, this is the case. But then people who don't like these results ask, how long does such an effect last? That is, experiments show that violent music primes people to more violent mental states immediately following the experiment. But should we care if then a half hour later the subjects are back to normal?

There is little or no research tackling this final question, unfortunately. But there are quite a few things we do know.

First, we know that if your kid listens to music with violent lyrics, you should take that as a potential warning sign of other potential trouble. There is a line to be drawn on this, however. I remember my friend's mother turning off the radio in the car once because she was so convinced her son listened to offensive music all the time (he did not listen to anything different than most of the rest of us). She turned off the radio because we were listening to The Who's "We're Not Gonna Take It" which has the word "rape" in it. But the music of The Who voiced teen angst and anxiety and never contained explicit lyrics demeaning women or promoting violence.

So what is determined to be bad music takes some work, for a parent has to delineate between traditional teen rebellion music and truly offensive music. Offensive music regularly treats women as objects, promotes violence, and glamorizes breaking the law. Teen rebellion music may occasionally say some unsavory things, but ultimately, offensive music is qualitatively and quantitatively different in that it is more explicit more often.

Negative Effects

The research on offensive music clearly shows negative effects. Researchers tend to focus on a small family of effects. First, research like that conducted by Barongan and Hall has found that people who regularly listen to heavy metal or rap music significantly score higher on measures of aggression and have a lower regard for women. They also generally mistrust others more than people who do not listen to this type of music. The differences are fairly modest, however. For example, people who regularly listen to heavy metal regard women about ten percent less than people who listen to other types of music. On the other hand, rap listeners have been found to score fifty percent higher on typical aggression scales compared to those who listen to adult contemporary, dance, soul, alternative, or country music. Listeners of heavy metal were not much better. And additionally, listeners of rap were found to be extremely distrustful, with heavy metal listeners a somewhat distant second. In fact, Snoop Dogg (rap) fans are nearly twice as distrustful of others than are listeners of Janet Jackson (dance/soul).

Furthermore, in other surveys, researchers found an association between listening to heavy metal or rap and below-average school grades, an increase in school behavior problems, sexual activity at a younger age, drug use, alcohol use, and even arrests. In this same survey, nearly half of heavy metal/rap listeners had below average grades, compared to a quarter of the other teens. The same difference was found for school suspensions. Heavy metal and rap listeners were found by Took to be twice as likely to be sexually active (participants in the study ranged from 12 to 18 years of age). More than twice as many heavy metal/rap listeners had been counseled for drugs or alcohol. Finally, nearly three times as many heavy metal/rap listeners used drugs than did other teenagers.

Rap Music and Its Effects

Indeed, the rap on rap goes much deeper. In one experiment by John, Jackson and Gatto, researchers randomly divided a group of males into three groups. One group watched violent rap music videos, another, nonviolent rap music videos, and a third, no videos at all. Then, everyone read two stories. In one, a couple meets an old friend of the woman in the couple. The friend kisses the woman, which leads to the man in the couple pushing his partner and punching the friend. Participants in the study were then asked if the man's behavior was justifiable. Then participants were read a second story, where two high school friends decide whether or not to go to college. One does decide to go to college (to become a lawyer) and one does not. When the college-bound person comes home for a visit, he finds his non-college friend wearing expensive clothes, driving an expensive car, etc. When asked where he got the money, the college-bound friend is told to not worry about it, but that the lesson was that kids don't have to go to college to get nice things. After this story, participants were asked which boy they would most want to be like.

Overall, participants who watched either type of rap video were much more likely to report that the man's violent reactions to both his girlfriend and her friend were justifiable. In fact, compared to people who did not watch any videos, they were nearly twice as likely to say the violence was justified. Furthermore, those who watched the violent videos were significantly more likely to say they would do the same thing in the same situation. And finally, as you might suspect, those who watched rap videos were much more likely to want to be more like the friend who did not go to college. And in fact, not only did they not want to be like the person who went to college, they also substantially downgraded his chances of one day becoming a successful lawyer, compared to participants in the experiment who did not watch rap videos.

It seems that part of the deleterious effect of rap and of heavy metal is not because of the music itself but the specific content of the music. For example, in an experiment by Barongan and Hall, people were divided into two groups, one where women were demeaned in rap music and one with other types of rap music. Participants were then given three film clips and asked to choose one and give it to a female researcher who was part of the experiment. The three films included one that contained a sexual rape, one that contained a sexual assault, and one that had no rape or assault. Participants who listened to rap that was sexually demeaning to women decided to show the non-sexually violent video clip seventy percent of the time. However, those who listened to non-demeaning rap chose the non-sexually violent clip ninety-three percent of the time. In short, those who listened to sexually demeaning rap were four times as likely to choose a clip with sexual violence than those who did not listen to sexually demeaning music.

So the point is, yes, offensive music can lead to bad choices. But a word of caution is that this does not mean that one should prohibit all rock music from being played in the house. What it does suggest is that parents need to know what their kids are listening to. Music does serve as a window into the soul. Your children listen to music that they think represents them, and that is an outward suggestion of what they are feeling inside. That said, most teenagers, are going through plenty of hormonal and social changes. I myself used to listen to and play jazz guitar since the seventh grade and ultimately ended up listening to some of the most nonviolent rock music out there (The Grateful Dead!). But I also had a heavy metal phase and owned every Iron Maiden album they had made at that time. So it can be tough for parents to judge whether a turn in musical tastes is a turn for the worse or just a temporary exploration of something different.

What to Do About It

Regardless, it is clear from the research that even good kids can be negatively impacted by bad music. Again, if you are concerned, the best way to deal with the issue is through open communication. But before you even attempt communication, be certain of what your kid is listening to. There are, after all, Christian bands who sound just like Metallica. Write down the names of the bands your kids listen to, then check them out on the Internet. Most lyrics are out there. Read them and make your own judgment.

If you find the content unsavory, ask your kid if they understand what their rock stars are saying. Ask if they agree. Ask if they realize how the views of their rock idols may be immoral or otherwise not what society needs. Demeaning their music or musical tastes is not a recipe for success. Giving them the seeds of rationality, and letting them come to their own realization about their music, will often yield better results.

That said, if your kid continues to play music incessantly that you feel demeans women and glamorizes violence, it could be a sign of something within. You will not be able to stop them from listening, since there are too many places outside of your control where they can listen. But if they do not understand your concerns, and the turn to bad music is also associated with a turn toward bad behavior, it may be time to seek professional help.

In summary, middle school kids are making their own choices about media, and your control over that is either already non-existent or largely curtailed. Thus, I strongly advocate the transition from control to inoculation. You may not be able to control what they watch and what they listen to, but you can reduce or entirely eliminate any negative effect media can have. Open communication is key; letting them know they can make their own decisions establishes the trust that opens up receptiveness to information about what they need to be aware of regarding potentially harmful effects of the media.

CHAPTER 6 CHEAT SHEET

TELEVISION AND MOVIES

KEY CONCERN	Sex and violence.
REMEDY	Inoculation, open discussion with your children.

INTERNET

KEY CONCERN	Sex.
REMEDY	Inoculation; open discussion with your children; better filtering and oversight.

MUSIC

KEY CONCERN	Violence and music degrading women.
REMEDY	Oversight, open discussion.

High School and Beyond

IN THINKING ABOUT how to start this chapter, I was struck by the common presidential slogan in the midst of a reelection campaign: "Four more years!" You have spent thirteen or fourteen years acting, at first, as the mediator between your children and media, and, then, as protector of them, and then, finally, as educator to them. There are only a few issues left to educate your children on in order to prepare them for a lifetime of living and interacting with mass media.

Party Time! Alcohol and the Media

A final topic on which there is significant research being conducted regards how we interact and live with the mass media and the concern that media exposure effects include:

1. Increased awareness of alcohol
2. If and why advertising alcohol is persuasive to kids
3. Whether exposure increases use
4. Whether parental mediation can reduce or eliminate the effect of alcohol exposure on their teenagers.

Alcohol Advertisements in Print and Televised Media

How much content is out there that contains in any way images or messages about alcohol? One study by Austin and Hust measured the top twenty-two magazines that target twelve to twenty-year-olds. They also looked at advertisements that were aired in a major U.S. city over a ten-week period. They found that when it comes to beverages, alcohol wins out, as more advertisements in both the magazines and the TV commercials were for alcoholic beverages than for nonalcoholic beverages.

Advertisements of Beverages

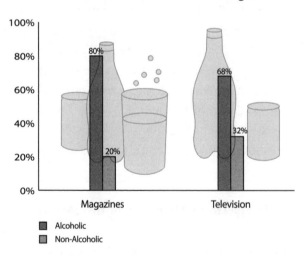

Source: Austin and Hust

Of course, in television, most ads are for beer. In magazines, however, one sees three ads for hard liquor for every one about beer or wine. And as you might expect from seeing hundreds of these commercials yourself, one of the notable findings in the research is that there are quite a lot of women being treated as objects, what researchers call sexual stereotyping (the stereotypical blond cheerleader in a beer commercial for example). Seventy percent of the magazine ads on alcohol contained sexual stereotyping of women, and the same was true for thirty percent of the women portrayed in television commercials. Few men are sexually stereotyped in these ads—just twelve percent for magazine ads and a whopping one and half percent in television ads. It is probably no surprise to you that the majority of the ads that exist in the top twenty-two magazines for teens and young adults are the same ads that are placed in the most popular magazines out there, including *Sports Illustrated*, *Rolling Stone*, and of course, *Playboy*. Beverage ads in these magazines are for alcoholic beverages over seventy-five percent of the time.

Since alcohol advertisements are most prevalent in media most consumed by youth, researchers have wondered why such advertising works so well.

In one study, teens were asked to rate commercials by their music, actors and actresses, animal characters, overall story, and humor. As noted by the authors, ads that contained a message about the legal drinking age and ads that primarily featured product characteristics were rated as less favorable than those using humor and storylines. Thus there is little reason to talk about the product in such commercials. The message of the research to alcohol advertisers is, sell the image, not the product.

As you might expect, teens notice these ads. Teens who consume a lot of television and magazines also happen to be more aware of and knowledgeable about alcohol. This includes not just knowledge of brand names and slogans, but also the successful ability to place a brand name into an ad whose brand name was whited out. No matter how the researchers looked at the data, there was a clear link between exposure to alcohol ads and awareness of them.

And now for the real question on your minds: Does it work? Surprisingly, the results are a bit mixed. One study by Stacy and colleagues measured alcohol use in the seventh grade and then recontacted the same teens a year later, in the eighth grade. They found that twenty-eight percent of seventh graders and thirty-four percent of eighth graders had drunk beer.

The researchers also found that if a teen was found to be a high consumer of television, especially television most likely to have commercials on alcohol, they had a greater likelihood to begin consuming alcohol in the following year than did teenagers with low or moderate television exposure. Overall, high consumers of TV were just under one and a half times more likely to initiate drinking than were low media consumers. However, another study by Ellickson and colleagues looking at the same kids across the eighth to ninth grade years found similar effects. But upon further research the effect of advertising was pushed aside in favor of other drivers of alcohol use, including social influences, social bonds with friends and family, and kids' behavioral history, including their tendency to be deviant or impulsive in the past. Indeed, the supposed effect of mass media appears to be a minor factor with regard to behavior. In short, your children are more likely to initiate drinking for a number of other reasons, from the personal to the social, than they are because they saw an advertisement for beer.

Many other studies that have explored the potential link between alcoholic advertising and behavior have similarly found mixed results. In fact, a somewhat dated review of the available literature found little impact at best.

Other researchers have studied the question of whether parental mediation has any impact at all on mediating what effect on knowledge and attitudes, and perhaps behavior, advertising of alcohol may have. Certainly, a host of studies have found that *general* monitoring of children regarding alcoholic consumption can be effective (regardless of whether they have been exposed to advertisements on alcohol or not). This is true not just for alcohol but drugs and cigarettes as well. But researchers have so far not been able to successfully determine whether monitoring and limiting of exposure to alcoholic advertisements is *specifically* effective.

Looking at the research on alcohol and the media, we thus generally find a weak link, if any link at all, with the exception of basic awareness of the brands and slogans. This book is not the space in which to discuss when it is okay for one's child to drink alcohol, or what to do about it when it happens. By the time they get to high school, somewhere around a third of kids will have already initiated consumption to some degree. Surely, if you suspect a problem, or you simply expect initiation at an age too early for your comfort, seek out information on what to do and consider your options before reacting.

TV and Movies: Values to Last a Lifetime

Earlier I talked about how one can conceive of television and mass media more generally as the village storyteller. In that early part of the book, we were concerned with the way media distorts our "knowledge" about the real world. We think, in short, that the real world is much more violent, more sexualized, and at least in some media, more filled with risky activities like cigarette smoking and alcoholic consumption. But more than that, the media offers us a set of values. And to some degree or another, we live our lives based on both the values of our everyday influences as well as the values of the characters, stories, and messages embedded in the mass media.

For one, it is thought that television, and the mass media more generally, glorifies the values of capitalism. Many researchers and noted scholars have spent a lifetime making this point and describing to us exactly how it happens.

Certainly, the classic message in America is that hard work is rewarded, and any American aspires to be rich. The media perpetuates this vision. Certainly, the people we see on television lead us to think that America is far more affluent than it really is. After all, for every ten lawyers being played as characters on shows or in advertisements on television, you probably only see one farmer or general laborer. And researchers have found that not only does television skew how rich we think the rest of America is, it also is linked to general approval of capitalist values, as heavy viewers report more support in capitalist systems than lighter viewers.

But beyond capitalism, our basic, general values that make up who we are as a society are influenced by the mass media as well. One researcher explored a number of specific values, including "good wins over evil," "truth always wins out," "relax, don't take things too seriously," "its better to be lucky than smart or strong," and "hard work yields good rewards." The study asked to what degree teenagers thought these and other themes were prevalent in the mass media. The teens were then asked how much television they watched, by the genre of program watched. In short, the researchers measured how much news kids watched compared to game shows, situation comedies, etc. All sorts of interesting results were found that clearly link media use to the values people associate with mass media. For example, those that reported that the media promotes the value of luck being important, also happened to score highly on the frequency of watching what type of show? You guessed it, game shows. How about "don't take things too seriously"? Heavy watchers of cartoons. Talk show viewers believe most that hard work is rewarding, no doubt since there are so many guests that underscore this theme. Sports scored similarly highly on this theme. How about "only the strong survive"? Interesting, high consumers of soap operas had not an attraction, but an aversion to believing this was true! Soap opera viewers, at least, did feel that in the end, the truth wins out.

Thus, as this study illustrates, we pick up messages from the mass media, whether we think this is true or not. The mass media is embedded in theme making and in storytelling. And every story has a moral and a message. Understanding this gives you leverage because you can now communicate this to your child. They can understand, as you do, that who we are and who we want to be is in part influenced by the mass media. If you think about people you have met in your past, you can probably think of people on both ends of the scale. In college I knew some guys who watched more television than I thought possible. It was not just on for five to six hours a day, but they were intently watching most of that time; it was not simply on in the background. On the other hand, I have had friends so driven by career and life in general that they never seemed to stop. Of the few friends I have had that are wired this way, not a single one of them has a television. There are just not enough hours in the day for them to be interested in sitting in front of a TV.

In short, media have a mainstreaming effect on us. It does, to a degree, lull us into a limited choice-set of how we act and think. Regardless of how much media your teenagers consume, it is important for them to understand this type of influence on them. It is subtle. But it can be powerful on some. By teaching them media literacy, and educating them on media effects, it is hoped they are better able to make up their own character, their own personality, without having to borrow one from the media. Because in the end, that is what we most want our kids to be: Somebody they decide to be.

Better for them to make up their minds themselves than via images they see in the media.

Computers and the Internet

We have reviewed quite a bit with regard to computers and the Internet thus far. But it is important to further review social networking, because in high school and beyond, kids are utilizing social networking more and more.

Social Networking Turns into Deep Social Relationships

In the last chapter we discussed the electronic social networking tendencies of today's teenagers. I noted the prevalence and type of media they use to communicate and project their personalities. As mentioned, electronic media is an excellent avenue for "trying out" various aspects of one's personality. In the high school years, such experimentation can occur more frequently. A recent study by Valkenburg, Schouten, and Peter, in fact, showed that half of all chat or instant message users at age eighteen have experimented with their identity on the Internet.

Why do they experiment? For one, electronic communication serves as a "test balloon" platform; it is ideal for such experimentation. Second, again as I have noted, the Internet tends to be an easier way to communicate for those with any level of social anxiety. Thus this research on eighteen-year-olds found that overcoming shyness was a motivator for experimenting with one's identity on the Internet. Finally, identity experimentation was used to teens' advantage, as the change in identity was meant to facilitate a social bond with another. Again, this is not so different than the type of thing kids will do face to face.

When kids experiment, what do they say they are (that they are not)? Nearly half of the kids in the study said they pretended to be a little older. And overall, about one out of ten provided at least one of the following changes: becoming more flirtatious than they are in real life, pretending to be someone's real life acquaintance, or pretending to be someone else entirely. Interestingly, boys report this complete "identity fantasy" experimenting about twice as often as girls.

But overall, kids are spending most of their time online being who they are. And their real relationships with others are becoming more involved as they get older. Nearly all online kids are interacting with their friends online. But what about developing relationships with people online, never to meet (yet) in person? And what about not just friend-of-friend acquaintances, but real friends with whom teens have shared the things they feel are important to them? Overall this number is generally low. One study by Wolak, Mitchell and Finkelhor found it to be about seven percent of online teens. Only two percent of these got intimate enough for that other person to be considered a boyfriend or girlfriend in the romantic sense, since as you might suspect such a development is difficult without some form of in-person contact. But nevertheless, it does occur, and specifically, fewer than one in three online but impersonal close relationships become romantic to some degree.

About a third of these relationships begins through some contact within one's friends or family. Three quarters of teens reported that their parents were aware of such relationships. And importantly, few teens report this to have been negative; nearly all such experiences have been reported as being positive.

Certainly, the closeness of online friends is generally perceived to be a step below in-person friends. Online friends do not get the advantage of time (in-person friends tend to have been around much longer), interactivity (you cannot play soccer with them, go to a movie with them, etc.), and quantity of communication (you can say a lot more to someone verbally than you can with a keyboard in the same amount of time). Nevertheless, as we have seen, the vast number of associations one has online are friends that one has met in-person as well. In fact, ninety-three percent of online close friends are also close friends in-person. And of these friends, research has found that the online environment makes them close, and improves the well-being of the relationship. The only negative effect of online communication on one's own sense of well-being is communication with strangers. Most research has found that teens who interact with strangers online report lower ratings of general life satisfaction. Of course, this is probably indicative of something else, and the likelihood to meet strangers online could be in part motivated by this dissatisfaction. Some research, however, does show less satisfaction with relationships with friends and family, though, so more study is needed.

As we discussed in the prior chapter, those with social anxiety can use the Internet as a less stressful mode of interaction than face-to-face interaction. And sure enough, in a study of teenagers, those with high social anxiety report higher online communication and self-disclosure of themselves online.

Overall, what is clear is that high schoolers are developing deeper electronic connections with their friends. From all the research, this should be considered normal for their generation. Clearly, online communication has its advantages and disadvantages, but overall, there should be no major concerns as your teen becomes more and more interconnected, not including what I have reviewed in earlier chapters regarding strangers, identity theft, sexual content, and so on.

Media Literacy

Reading this book has hopefully been a catalyst for you to understand and teach your kids media literacy. For media literacy means a number of things, and the first thing it means is to become knowledgeable about what the media has been shown to do to children and adults alike, specifically what impact it has on our knowledge about reality, our attitudes about reality, and our behaviors in the everyday world. One cannot teach kids about the mass media without understanding it. So though you probably bought this book to protect and teach your kids about the media, what you have done first and foremost is taught yourself quite a bit about the media, how it interacts with people, influences, and affects them. By passing on this knowledge to your kids, you are conducting media literacy. You are giving them knowledge, and knowledge is power.

So in wrapping up this book, this survival guide for parents on the mass media, I think it is important to review the lessons you have learned. Because these are the same lessons you should be passing on to your children. These are the lessons they should pass along to their children as well. What have we learned? In sum:

1. *How Much Matters:* The more television really young children watch, the more likely they are to develop negative outcomes, from attention problems (to some degree) or aggression. In older kids, the more they watch, the more they believe the world is mean, sexual, and violent—and the more they accept "television values" rather than the values passed on by their parents.
2. *Television Can Educate:* But remember, it's the type of television that matters.

3. *Kids Should Never Have a Television in Their Bedroom:* Plain and simple.

4. *Music Is Good for the Soul:* At least, good music for young children.

5. *Music Is As Persuasive, If Not More So, Than Other Media:* Violent music is associated with violent tendencies to some extent. Music degrading women can lower adolescent boys' regard for women.

6. *Computers Can Teach:* Despite the few who want kids to play outside all day, studies show computers can have quite positive educational impact.

7. *Advertising Works:* Young children have no defenses. Parents need to build these defenses at early ages, as soon as kids are cognitively complex enough to understand.

8. *The Media Is Violent:* Quite a bit of adult programming is violent, and depending on how violence is defined, kids programs can be even more violent. Use the ratings systems, filtering, and V-chip to limit exposure.

9. *The Internet Is Not Awash in Pornography, but Nevertheless Kids Need Protection:* Learn to use that filtering software and continually teach yourself the latest tricks and strategies to protect your kids from unsavory content.

10. *Video Games Can Teach:* They can teach hand-eye skills, and they can teach that violence is normal. Make sure you mediate the types of games your kids play.

11. *Media Can Nudge Kids to Drink and Smoke:* Positive messages on drinking and smoking can impact your kids. Have a talk with them about these subjects before they see such messages in the media.

12. *All Media Can Be Addictive:* Television, video games, the Internet, and computers can all be over used. If there is one behavior that will bring out the worst in what media teaches kids, it is addictive behavior.

13. *Your Teens Will Meet a LOT of People Online:* Friends, acquaintances, and possibly, predators and identity thieves. Online interaction is normal, just make sure your kids know who to stay away from online and what not to reveal (personal information).

14. *Media Literacy Can Make People Smarter:* Media literacy teaches critical thinking. It allows people to live lives unchained: They can make up their own minds about things rather than be beholden to the influence of mass media. And, media literacy and critical thinking can teach kids to be more analytical in everyday life.

You have, in short, learned quite a bit! The last lesson to learn is how to continue pushing yourself and your kids with regard to being literate and critical of the mass media. Importantly, to be critical does not mean to be necessarily negative. Media are meant to be enjoyed, not villified. What the term critical means here is to always be aware, to always question and think through the messages you are presented with via the mass media. Entertainment media are largely designed in such a way that you are encouraged not to think about them. Dissecting them is too much work, for something you often consume in order to turn everything off and vegetate.

What is the best way to get from being an awkward media critic to an automatic media critic? The first is to train yourself to think constantly about a limited number of questions one might ask about media as they watch, show by show, in order to better understand it and understand the latent messages embedded within. These include:

1. What is being promoted by this media? Specifically, what attitudes and values are being promoted as good, and should they be?

2. Are people in particular and society in general being accurately portrayed? How not, and what is the impact of this?
3. What is being lusted after in media programming? Specifically, what do the characters want and how do they go about getting it?
4. How is mood and emotion created via the setting, the lighting, the camera angles, etc.?
5. How might other people interpret differently what you are watching, based on their different heritages, values, and upbringing?

As you and your teens continually think about these questions from show to show, you will start to notice that you think of these questions more frequently without prompting, without having to consciously think about them. When this starts to happen, it is a sign that you are becoming a critical consumer of media. And the point is to get to a place where you don't have to work hard to be critical—it comes naturally.

By talking to your kids about media literacy, and having conversations with them that revolve around these critical questions, your kids will also begin to become natural critical consumers of media. They will become in charge of their own lives, rather than being led by the latest fad or imbedded value system broadcast in the media.

Media and Life

Media are here to stay, in case you have not figured that out yet. We live our lives consuming media everyday, and quite a lot of it. Media is not inherently bad. Media can have bad content. Bad people are out there as characters in a movie and

as predators online. Media have become our village storytell-
ers. But this is not all bad. For as many dumb stories that are
told on television, I think there are just as many told in books.
Remember that media have a lot to offer. Good stories. Good
morals. Lessons. Knowledge. The goal of this book, unlike
quite a few that are out there, is not to completely unplug
your kids. Indeed, the title is really half of a sentence, and that
sentence is, unplug your kids when you can, and protect them
from it when you can't. It is not possible, nor it is really favorable, to completely unplug your kids. To do so would put them
at a disadvantage in today's plugged-in world. Rather, let them
stay plugged in, but not all the time, and not with the unsavory
elements that are offered in each of the major types of media.
As your kids get older, educate them about media. Inoculate
them so that when they are plugged in they shed off the bad
messages and bad potential influences and maximize the good.

Parents do not have to be super parents. But since we all
live in this fishbowl called media, it behooves us all to learn
about them, to separate their good contributions to society
from the bad. You pass on that learning to your kids so they
can live reflexive lives, that is, lives in which they are in control, and media are not an undue influence.

This has been a book based on research. I do not say any
of the above because I walked into writing this book with an
opinion. However, research only goes so far. Scientists have
only figured out a significant but still small amount of what
media can and cannot do. But moving away from the trees
to look at the forest for a second, it is clear that the research
reveals two essential and indubitable facts about living and
raising kids in a world of mass media. Everything in moderation, and knowledge is power. Live your lives, and raise your
kids, with these two guidelines, and you are likely assured a
productive life living in this village we call the mass media.

CHAPTER 7 CHEAT SHEET

TELEVISION AND MOVIES

KEY CONCERN

Attitudes toward and use of alcohol.

REMEDY

Inoculation, open discussion with your children.

ADVERTISING AND MEDIA LITERACY

KEY CONCERN

Media influence on values and thinking.

REMEDY

Advanced media literacy.

References

Anderson, C., & Bushman, B. (2001). Effects of violent video games on aggressive behavior, aggressive cognition, aggressive affect, physiological arousal, and prosocial behavior: a meta-analytic review of the scientific literature. *Psychological Science*, 12: 353-365.

Anderson, C. A. (2004). An update on the effects of playing violent video games. *Journal of Adolescence*. 27: 113-122.

Anderson, C.; Berkowitz, L.; Donnerstein, E.; Rowell Huesmann, L.; Johnson, J.; & Linz, D. (2003). *The Influence of Media Violence on Youth*. 4: 81-110.

Anderson, D.R.; Bryant, J.; Wilder, A.; Santomero, A.; Williams, M.; & Crawley, A. M. (2000). Researching *Blue's Clues*: Viewing Behavior and Impact. *Media Psychology*, 2: 179-194.

Anderson, J., & Wilkins, R. (1998). *Getting Unplugged: Take Control of Your Family's Television, Video Game, and Computer Habits.* New York, NY: John Wiley and Sons.

Arnon, Samuel (June 2006). Live music is beneficial to preterm infants in the neonatal intensive care unit environmental. *Birth.* 33: 131-135.

Are cell phones safe? *Consumer Reports,* Feb. 2003, 68: 24.

Austin, E. W., and Hust, S. J. T. (2005). Targeting adolescents? The content and frequency of alcoholic and nonalcoholic beverage ads in magazine and video formats November 1999-April 2000. *Journal of Health Communication,* 10: 769-785.

Austin, E.; Pinkleton, B.; & Fujioka, Yuki (2000). The Role of Interpretation Processes and Parental Discussion in the Media's Effects on Adolescents' Use of Alcohol. *Pediatrics.* 105: 343-349.

Baird, A. L., and Grieve, F. G. (2006). Exposure to male models in advertisements leads to a decrease in men's body satisfaction. *North American Journal of Psychology,* 8: 115-122.

Bandyopadhyay, S., Kindra, G., & Sharp, L. (2001). Is television advertising good for children? Areas of concern and policy implications. *International Journal of Advertising.* 20: 89-116.

Bankart, C. P., & Anderson, C. (1979). Short-term effects of pro-social television viewing on play of preschool boys and girls. *Psychological Reports,* 44: 935-941.

Bartholow, B.; Sestir, M.; & Davis, E. (Nov. 2005). Correlates and Consequences of Exposure to Video Game Violence: Hostile Personality, Empathy, and Aggressive Behavior. *Personality and Social Psychology Bulletin.* 31: 1573-1586.

Bauserman, Robert (1996). Sexual Aggression and Pornography: A Review of Correlational Research. *Basic and Applied Social Psychology.* 18: 405-427.

REFERENCES

Bergler, R. (1999). The effects of commercial advertising on children. *International Journal of Advertising*, 18: 411–425.

Blaine County School District No. 61. Computer Skills: 2006 Curriculum Information Packet.

Blumberg, Fran C. & Sokol, Lori, M. (2004). Boys' and Girls' Use of Cognitive Strategy When Learning to Play Video Games. *The Journal of General Psychology.* 131: 151–158.

Bolis, P., Chen, C., and Popeski, W. (2003). Sex and violence makes me yawn: Autonomic desensitization to music videos. International Communication Association Annual Meeting, 1–5.

Bryant, J., & Bryant, J. A. (2001). *Television and the American Family (2nd ed.).* Mahway, NJ: Lawrence Erlbaum Associates.

Buckleitner, W. (2007). Is this game OK to play? *Scholastic Parent and Child,* April.

Buijzen, Moniek, & Valkenburg, Patti M. (2003). The effects of television advertising on materialism, parent–child conflict, and unhappiness: A review of research. *Applied Developmental Psychology.* 24: 437–56.

Carlson, James (1993). Television Viewing: Cultivating Perceptions of Affluence and Support for Capitalist Values. *Political Communication.* 10: 243–257.

Casanova, Manuel F. Solursh, Diane Solursh, Lionel Roy, Emil; & Thigpen, Lance. The history of child pornography on the Internet. *Journal of Sex Education and Therapy,* 25: 245–51.

Cell phone trackers: Now parents can track their kids with cell phones. Is this technology a good thing? *Scholastic Scope,* (September 4, 2006), p. 18.

Certain, Kahn, (2002). Prevalence, Correlations, and Trajectory of Television Viewing Among Infants and Toddlers. *Pediatrics.* 109: 634-642.

Cheng, T.; Brenner, R.; Wright, J.; Sachs, H.; Moyer, P.; & Rao, M. (2004). Children's Violent Television Viewing: Are Parents Monitoring? *Pediatrics,* 114: 94-99.

Cho, C., & Cheon, H. J. (2005). Children's exposure to negative Internet content: Effects of family context. *Journal of Broadcasting and Electronic Media,* 49: 488-509.

Christakis, D. A., & Zimmerman, F. J. (2006). *The Elephant in the Living Room: Make Television Work for Your Kids.* New York: Rodale.

Christakis, D. A., & Zimmerman, F. J. (2007). Violent television viewing during preschool is associated with antisocial behavior during school age. *Pediatrics,* 19: 993-999.

Christakis, D., & Zimmerman, F. (2004). Early Television Exposure and Subsequent Attentional Problems in Children. *Pediatrics,* 113: 708-713.

Christakis, D.A; Ebel, B.E.; Rivara, F.P.; & Zimmerman, F.J. (2004). Television, video, and computer game usage in children under 11 years of age. *The Journal of Pediatrics,* 145: 652-658.

Clements, D. H. (1987). Computers and young children: A review of research. *Young Children,* "November": 34-44.

Clements, D. H. (1997). Effective Use of Computers with Young Children. In: Mathematics in the early years. Copley, Juanita V.; Washington, DC, U.S.: National Association for the Education of Young Children, 1999. pp. 119-128.

CMCH suggestions: Practice media literacy (2007). *www.cmch .tv/mentors_parents/tips_media_literacy_thinking.asp.*

Cohen, A. (2006). Do you know where your kids are clicking? *PC Magazine,* July, 88-96.

Collins, R. L.; Elliott, M. N.; Berry, S. H.; et al. (2004). Watching sex on television predicts adolescent initiation of sexual behavior. *Pediatrics,* 114: e280-e289.

Collins, R. L.; Schell, T.; Ellickson, P. L.; & McCaffrey, D. (2003). Predictors of beer advertising awareness among eighth graders. *Society for the Study of Addiction to Alcohol and Other Drugs,* 98: 1297-1306.

Committee on Communications, (2006). Children, adolescents, and advertising. *American Academy of Pediatrics.* 118: 2563-69.

Committee on Communications, (2006). Children, Adolescents, and Advertising. *Pediatrics.* 118: 2563-2567.

Crawley, A. M.; Anderson, D. R.; Santomero, A.; et al. (2002). Do children learn how to watch television? The impact of extensive experience with *Blue's Clues* on preschool childrens' television viewing behavior. *Journal of Communication,* 52: 264-280.

Cryan, J. R. (1984). Children and TV: The ABCs of TV Literacy. *Childhood Education.* 201-205.

Custodero, Lori A. (2003). Musical lives: A collective portrait of American parents and their young children. *Applied Developmental Psychology.* 24: 553-572.

Dalton, Madeline D.; Sargent, James D.; & Beach, Michael L.; et al. (2003). Effect of viewing smoking in movies on adolescent smoking initiation: a cohort study. *The Lancet.* 362: 281-286.

DeBell, Matthew, & Chapman, Chris (2003). Computer and Internet use by children and adolescents in 2001. National Center for Education Statistics.

Dennison, A., & Jenkins, L. (2002). Television Viewing and Television in Bedroom Associated with Overweight Risk Among Low-Income Preschool Children. *Pediatrics.* 109: 1028-1035.

Dennison, B.; Erb, T.; & Jenkins, P. (2002). Television viewing and television in bedroom associated with overweight risk among low-income preschool children. *Pediatrics.* 109: 1028-1035.

Dietz, W., & Gortmaker, S. (1985). Do we fatten our children at the television set? Obesity and television viewing in children and adolescents. *Pediatrics.* 75: 807-812.

Din, F., & Calao, J. (2001). The Effects of Playing Educational Video Games on Kindergarten Achievement. *Child Study Journal.* 31: 95-102.

Donohue, T. R.; Henke, L. L.; & Donohue, W. A. (1980). Do kids know what TV commercials intend? *Journal of Advertising Research.* 20: 51-57.

Drabman, R., & Hannratty Thomas, M. (1977). Children's imitation of aggressive and prosocial behavior when viewing alone and in pairs. *Journal of Communication,* 27: 199-204.

Dunnewind, S. Where the world virtually revolves around kids; More and more websites are catering to younger children, with avatars, "pets," safety features and sometimes, lots of ads. (2007, February 10). *The Seattle Times Company,* p. C1.

Eagle, L. (2007). Commercial media literacy: What does it do, to Whom, and Does it matter? *Journal of Advertising,* 36: 101-110.

Eastin, M. S., & Greenberg, B. S. (2007). Parenting the Internet. *Journal of Communication,* 56: 486-504.

Eggert, J.; Levendosky, A.; & Klump, K. (2006). Relationships among attachment styles, personality characteristics, and disordered eating. *International Journal of Eating Disorders.* 40: 149-155.

Ellickson, P. L.; Collins, R. L.; Hambarsoomians, K.; & McCaffrey, D. F. (2005). Does alcohol advertising promote adolescent drinking? Results from a longitudinal assessment. *Society for the Study of Addiction,* 100: 235-246.

Fetler, M. (1984). Television Viewing and School Achievement. *Journal of Communication.* 34: 104-118.

Finkelhor, David; Mitchell, Kimberly J.; & Wolak, Janis (2000). Online victimization: a report on the nation's youth. National Center for Missing and Exploited Children.

Fisch, S. M.; Truglio, R. T.; & Cole, C. F. (1999). The impact of *Sesame Street* on preschool children: a review and synthesis of 30 years' research. *Media Psychology.* 1: 165-190.

Fisher, Sue (1994). Identifying video game addiction in children and adolescents. *Addictive Behaviors.* 19: 545-53.

Fleming, M. J., & Rickwood, D. J. (2001). Effects of Violent Versus Nonviolent Video Games on Children's Arousal, Aggressive Mood, and Positive Mood. *Journal of Applied Social Psychology.* [2047-2071].

Fleming, Michele J.; Greentree, Shane; Cocotti-Muller, Dayana; Elias, Kristy A.; & Morrison, Sarah (2006). Safety in cyberspace. *Youth & Society.* 38: 135-154.

Freeman-Longo, R. E. (2000). Children, teens, and sex on the Internet. *Sexual Addiction and Compulsivity,* 7: 75-90.

Friedman, Samuel J. (2000). *Children of the World Wide Web: Tool or Trap?* Lenham, Maryland: University Press of America, Inc.

Funk, J. B.; Baldacci, H. B.; Pasold, T.; & Baumgardner, J. (2004). Violence exposure in real-life, video games, television, movies, and the Internet: is there desensitization? *Journal of Adolescence,* 27: 23-39.

Garofoli, J. (2007, May 27). I'm 8, I'm late for an online date with a cuddly penguin. *The San Francisco Chronicle,* p. A1.

Geist, A., & Gibson. The Effect of Network and Public Television Programs on Four and Five Year Old Ability to Attend to Educational Tasks. *Journal of Instructional Psychology.* 27: 250-262.

Gentile, D. A. (ed). *Media Violence and Children: A Complete Guide for Parents and Professionals* (2003). Westport, CT: Praeger.

Gentile, D. A.; Lynch, P. J.; Linder, J. R.; & Walsh, D. A. (2004). The effects of violent video game habits on adolescent hostility, aggressive behaviors, and school performance. *Journal of Adolescence,* 27: 5-22.

Gillespie, Robin M. (2002). The physical impact of computers and electronic game use on children and adolescents, a review of current literature. IOS Press. 249-259.

Goldberg, M. E., & Gorn, G. J. (1978). Some unintended consequences of TV advertising to children. *Journal of Consumer Research.* 5: 22-29.

Goodstein, A. (2007). *Totally Wired: What Teens and Tweens are Really Doing Online.* New York, NY: St. Martin's Griffin.

Goodwin, L. D.; Goodwin, W. L.; Nansel, A.; & Helm, C. (1986). Cognitive and affective effects of various types of microcomputer use by preschoolers. *American Educational Research Journal,* 23: 348-356.

Gortmaker, S. L.; Must, A.; Sobol, A.M.; Peterson, K.; Colditz, G. A.; & Dietz, W. H. (1996). Television Viewing as a Cause of Increasing Obesity Among Children in the United States, 1986-1990. 150, [356-361].

Gortmaker, Steven L.; Salter, Charles A.; Walker, Deborah K.; & Dietz, William H. (1990). The impact of television viewing on mental aptitude and achievement: a longitudinal study. *Public Opinion Quarterly,* 54: 594-604.

Greenfield, P. M. (2004). Inadvertent exposure to pornography on the Internet: Implications of peer-to-peer file-sharing networks for child development and families. *Applied Developmental Psychology,* 25: 741-750.

Griffiths, M. (2000). Internet addiction—time to be taken seriously? *Addiction Research,* 8: 413-418.

Gross, Juvonen; Gable, Elisheva F.; Jaana, Shelly (2002). Internet Use and Well-Being in Adolescence. *Journal of Social Issues.* 58: 75-90.

Grusser, S. M.; Thalemann, R.; & Griffiths, M. D. (2007). Excessive Computer Game Playing: Evidence for Addiction and Aggression. *CyberPsychology & Behavior,* 10: 290-291.

Gunter, B.; Furnham, A.; & Griffiths, S. (2000). Children's memory for news: A comparison of three presentation media. *Media Psychology,* 2: 93-118.

Hall Hansen, Christine, & Hansen, Ronald D. (1990). Rock music videos and antisocial behavior. *Basic and Applies Social Psychology*, 11: 357-369.

Hansen, F. (2002). *Children: Consumption, Advertising, and Media.* Copenhagen: Copenhagen Business School Press.

Harrison, K., & Hefner, V. (2006). Media exposure, current and future body ideals, and disordered eating among preadolescent girls: a longitudinal panel study. *Journal of Youth and Adolescence.* 35: 153-163.

Haugland, S. W. (1999). What role should technology play in young children's learning? *Young Children,* November, 26-31.

Hawkins, N.; Richard, P.; Granley, H.; & Stein, D. (2004). The impact of exposure to the thin-ideal media image on women. *Eating Disorders,* 12: 35-50.

Henderson, R. W., and Rankin, R. J. (1986). Preschoolers' viewing of instructional television. *Journal of Educational Psychology,* 78: 44-51.

Hithchings, E., & Moynihan, P. J. (1998). The relationship between television food advertisements recalled and actual foods consumed by children. *Journal of Human Nutrition and Dietetics.* 11: 511-517.

Hoffmann, G. (1999). Media Literacy Study. *ETC: A Review of General Semantics,* 56: 165-171.

Hofmann, R. J., and Flook, M. A. (1980). An experimental investigation of the role of television in facilitating shape recognition. *Journal of Genetic Psychology,* 136: 305-306.

Hough, K. J., & Erwin, P. G. (1997). Children's attitudes toward violence on television. *The Journal of Psychology,* 131: 441-415.

Hunley, S. A.; Evans, J. H.; Delgado-Hachey, M.; et al. (2005). Adolescent computer use and academic achievement. *Adolescence*, 40: 307–318.

Hunter, Bryan C. (June 2006). Music for very young ears. *Birth*. 33: 137–138.

Iannotta, J. (2001). Nontechnical strategies to reduce children's exposure to inappropriate material on the Internet. 50–63.

Jackson, P. (2003). New initiatives to promote media literacy in children. *British Nutrition Foundation*. 28: 47–51.

Jackson, R. (2007). How to confront children using pornography. *www.family.org/lifechallenges/A000000219.cfm*.

Johnson, J.; Cohen, P.; Smailes, E.; Kasen, S.; & Brook, J. (2002). Television Viewing and Aggressive Behavior During Adolescence and Adulthood. *Reports*. 295: 2468– 2471.

Johnson, James D.; Jackson, Lee Anderson; & Gatto, Leslie (1995). Violent attitudes and deferred academic aspirations: deleterious effects of exposure to rap music. *Basic and Applied Social Psychology*. 16: 27–41.

Kaiser family Foundation (1998). National Surveys of Parents and Children. Washington, DC: Kaiser Family Foundation.

Kaiser Family Foundation (2002). Key Facts: Children and Video Games. Washington, DC. Kaiser Family Foundation.

Kaiser Family Foundation (2003). Issue brief: The Role of Media in Childhood Obesity. Washington, DC. Kaiser Family Foundation.

Kaiser Family Foundation (2003). Key Facts: Media Literacy. Washington, DC. Kaiser Family Foundation.

Kaiser Family Foundation (2003). Key Facts: TV Violence. Washington, DC. Kaiser Family Foundation.

Kaiser Family Foundation (2007). Food for Thought: Television Food Advertising to Children in the U.S. Washington, DC: Kaiser Family Foundation.

Kaiser, Henry J. (2002). Teens Online. From *www.kff.com*.

Kaltiala-Heino, R.; Lintonen, T.; & Rimpela, A. (2004). Internet Addiction? Potentially problematic use of the Internet in a population of 12-18 year-old adolescents. *Addiction Research and Theory.* 12: [89-96].

Kenway, J., & Bullen, E. (2001). *Consuming Children: Education—Entertainment—Advertising.* Philadelphia, PA: Open University Press.

Kirsh, S. J.; Olczak, P. V.; & Mounts, J. R. W. (2005). Violent Video Games Induce an Affect Processing Bias. *Media Psychology.* 7: 239-250.

Konrad, W. (2007). It's 2007; do you know where your kids are? *Good Housekeeping,* 244: 148-214.

Krahe, B., & Moller, I. (2004). Playing violent electronic games, hostile attributional style, and aggression-related norms in German adolescents. *Journal of Adolescence.* 27: 53-69.

Kronenberger, W. G.; Mathews, V. P.; Dunn, D. W.; et al. (2004). Media violence exposure and executive functioning in aggressive and control adolescents. *Journal of Clinical Psychology,* 61: 725-727.

Kubey, R. (1999). What is media literacy and why is it important? *Television Quarterly,* 21-27.

Kunkel, D., Eyal, K. (2005). The effects of sex on television's drama shows on emerging adults' sexual attitudes and moral judgments. International Communication Association, 2005 Annual Meeting, New York, NY, p. 1-44.

Lenhart, Amanda (2001). *www.pewinternet.org*. Retrieved November 20, 2007, from Pew Internet & American Life Project web site.

Lenhart, Amanda (2005, March, 17). Protecting teens online. Pew Internet & American Life Project.

Lenhart, Amanda (2007). Cyberbullying and online teens. Pew Internet & American Life Project.

Leone, R. (2004). Rated sex: An analysis of the MPAA's use of the R and NC-17 ratings. *Communication Research Reports*, 21: 68-74.

Levin, S.R., Petros, T.V., & Petrella, F.W. (1982). Preschoolers' Awareness of Television Advertising. *Child Development*. 53: 933-937.

Li, Xiaoming, & Atkins, Melissa S. (2004). Early childhood computer experience and cognitive and motor development. *Official Journal of the American Academy of Pediatrics*. 113: 1715-1722.

Liebert, R. M., & Sprafin, J. (2003). *The Early Window: Effects of Television on Children and Youth*. New York, NY: Pergamon Press.

Linebarger, D. L. (2001). Learning to read from television: The effects of using captions and narration. *Journal of Educational Psychology*, 93: 288-298.

Linz, Daniel G.; Donnerstein, Edward; & Penrod, Steven (1988). Effects of Long-Term Exposure to Violent and Sexually Degrading Depictions of Women. *Journal of Personality and Social Psychology*. 55: 758-768.

Livingstone, S., Bober, M. (2005). Taking up online opportunities? Children's uses of the Internet for education, communication, and participation. International Communication Association, 2005 Annual Meeting, New York, NY, p. 1-34.

Livingstone, S., & Helsper, E. J. (2006). Does Advertising Literacy Mediate the Effects of Advertising on Children? A Critical Examination of Two Linked Research Literatures in Relation to Obesity and Food Choice. *Journal of Communication*. 56: 560-584.

Livingstone, Sonia (2001). Children On-line: Emerging Uses of the Internet at Home. *Journal of the IBTE*. 2: 1-7.

Macklin, M. C. (1983). Do children understand TV ads? *Journal of Advertising Research*. 23: 63-70.

Macklin, M. C. (1985). Do young children understand the selling intent of commercials? *The Journal of Consumer Affairs*. 19: 293-304.

Macklin, M. C. (1987). Preschoolers' Understanding of the Informational Function of Television Advertising. *Journal of Consumer Research*. 14: 229-239

Macklin, M.C. (1990). The Influence of Model Age on Children's Reactions to Advertising Stimuli. *Psychology & Marketing*. 7: 295-310.

Macklin, M.C. (1994). The Effects of an Advertising Retrieval Cue on Young Children's Memory and Brand Evaluations. *Psychology & Marketing*. 11: 291-311.

Marshall, S.; Biddle, S.; Gorely, T.; Cameron, N.; & Murdey, I. (2004). Relationships between media use, body fatness and physical activity in children and youth: a meta-analysis. *Pediatric Highlight*. 28: 1238-1246.

McCabe, M.; & Ricciardelli, L. (2004). Body image dissatisfaction among males across the lifespan, a review of past literature. *Journal of Psychosomatic Research.* 56: 675-685.

Mesch, G., & Talmud, I. (2006). The Quality of Online and Offline Relationships: The Role of Multiplexity and Duration of Social Relationships. *The Information Society.* 22: 137-148.

Messerly, J. G. (2004). How Computer Games Affect CS (and Other) Students' School Performance. *Viewpoint.* 47: 29-31.

Mierlo, J. V., & Van de Bulck, J. (2003). Benchmarking the cultivation approach to video game effects: a comparison of the correlates of TV viewing and game play. *Journal of Adolescence.* 27: 97-111.

Mitchell, Denise R., & Dunbar, Carol A. (2006). Learning and development in the nursery setting: The value of promoting emergent information and communications technology skills. *Child Care in Practice.* 12: 241-257.

Mitchell, K., Finkelhor, D., & Wolak, J. (2005). Protecting youth online: Family use of filtering and blocking software. *Child Abuse and Neglect,* 29: 753-765.

Mitchell, S. (2007). Penguins and plagiarism: Stemming the tide of plagiarism in elementary school. *Library Media Connection.* 25: 47.

Moss, Linda (2006). New Net Caters to infants. Multichannel News, p. Top Stories.

Muris, P.; Merckelbach, H.; Gadat, B.; & Moulaert, V. (2000). Fears, worries, and scary dreams in 4 to 12-year-old children: Their content, developmental pattern and origins. *Journal of Clinical Child Psychology,* 29: 43-52.

Nathanson, Amy I. (2002). The Unintended Effects of Parental Mediation of Television on Adolescents. *Mediapsychology.* 4: 207-230.

Nikken, P., & Jansz, J. (2006). Parental mediation of children's videogame playing: a comparison of the reports by parents and children. *Learning, Media and Technology.* 31: 181-202.

Oster, A. (2005). The effect of introducing computers on children's problem-solving skills in science. *British Journal of Educational Technology*, 36: 907- 909.

Page, R. M. (1998). College students' distorted perception of the prevalence of smoking. *Psychological Reports.* 82: 474.

Pardun, C. J. ; l'Engle, K. L. ; & Brown, J. D. (2005). Linking exposure to outcomes: Early adolescents' consumption of sexual content in six media. *Mass Communication and Society,* 8: 75-91.

Parkinson, K.; Tovee, M.; & Cohen-Tovee, E. (1998). Body shape perceptions of preadolescent and young adolescent children. *European Eating Disorders Review.* 6: 126-135.

PBS parents guide to children and media (2007). *www.pbs. org/parents/chidlrenandmedia.* Persky, S., & Blascovich, J. (2007). Immersive Virtual Environments Versus Traditional Platforms: Effects of Violent and Nonviolent Video Game Play. *Media Psychology.* 10: 135-156.

Peter, J., & Valkenburg, P. M. (2006). Adolescents' exposure to sexually explicit online material and recreational attitudes toward sex. *Journal of Communication,* 56: 639-660.

Pine, K. J.; & Nash, A. (2002). Dear Santa: The effects of television advertising on young children. *International Journal of Behavioral Development.* 26: 529-539.

Pingree, S. (1986). Children's Activity and Television Comprehensibility. *Communication Research.* 13: 239–246.

Potter, W. J. (2003). *The 11 Myths of Media Violence.* Thousand Oaks, CA: Sage.

Predator tip sheet (2006). *www.isafe.org.*

Protect yourself online (2007). *Consumer Reports,* September, 28–45.

Puente, M. Babies, boomers join circle; Social networking sites go to the age extremes. (2007, June 18). *USA Today,* p. D7.

Ravitch, D., & Viteritti, J. (2003). *Marketing Sex and Violence to America's Children.* Baltimore & London: The Johns Hopkins University Press.

Reifinger Jr, James L. (2006). Skill Development in Rhythm Perception and Performance: A Review of Literature. Applications of Research in Music Education, 25, Retrieved August 2, 2007, from *http://navigator-wcupa.passhe.edu.*

Repacholi, M., & Ahlbom, A. (1999). Link Between Electromagnetic Fields and Childhood Danger Unresolved. *The Lancet.* 354: 1918–1919.

Ricciardelli, L., & McCabe, M. (2001). Children's body image concerns and eating disturbance: a review of the literature. *Clinical Psychology Review.* 21: 325–343.

Rich, M. (2005). Sex screen: The dilemma of media exposure and sexual behavior. *Pediatrics,* 116: 329–331.

Rubin, A. M.; West, D.V.; & Mitchell, W. S. (2001). Differences in aggression, attitudes toward women, and distrust as reflected in popular music preferences. *Media Psychology,* 3: 25–42.

Sanders, Christopher E.; Field, Tiffany M.; Diego, Miguel; & Kaplan, Michele (2000). The relationship of Internet use to depression and social isolation among adolescents. *Adolescence,* 35: 138.

Saplolsky, B. S., and Tabarlet, J. O. (1991). Sex in primetime television: 1979 versus 1989. *Journal of Broadcasting and Electronic Media,* 35.

Savage, L. (2007). Is Big Bird bad for Baby? *Maclean's,* 120: 46-47.

Scantlin, R., & Jordan, A. (2006). Families' Experiences with the V-chip: An Exploratory Study. *The Journal of Family Communication,* 6: 139-159.

Schutz, H. & Paxton, S. (2007). Friendship quality, body dissatisfaction, dieting and disordered eating in adolescent girls. *British Journal of Clinical Psychology.* 46: 67-83.

Segan, Sascha (2006). Cell phones and services for kids. *PC Magazine,* 40-1.

Shariff, I., & Sargent, J. D. (2006). Association between television, movie, and video game exposure and school performance. *Pediatrics,* 118: e1061-e1070.

Singer, D. G., & Singer, J. L. (1998). Developing Critical Viewing Skills and Media Literacy in Children. *The Annals of the American Academy.* 557: 164-179.

Slater, M. D. (2003). Alienation, aggression, and sensation seeking as predictors of adolescent use of violent film, computer, and website content. *Journal of Communication,* 53: 105-120.

Slater, M. D.; Henry, K. L.; Swaim, R. C.; & Anderson, L. L. (2003). Violent media content and aggressiveness in adolescents: A downward spiral. *Communication Research,* 30: 713-736.

Smith, S. L., & Wilson, B. J. (2002). Children's comprehension of and fear reactions to television news. *Media Psychology,* 4: 1-26.

Somers, C. L., & Tynan, J. J. (2006). Consumption of sexual dialogue and content on television and adolescent sexual outcomes: Multiethnic findings. *Adolescence,* 41: 15- 38.

Sprafkin, J. N.; Liebert, R. M.; & Poulos, R. W. (1975). Effects of a prosocial televised example on children's helping. *Journal of Experimental Child Psychology,* 20: 119-126.

Stacy, A. W.; Zogg, J. B.; Unger, J. B.; & Dent, C. W. (2004). Exposure to televised alcohol ads and subsequent adolescent alcohol use. *American Journal of Health Behavior,* 28: 498-509.

Steyer, James (2002). *The Other Parent.* New York, NY: Atria Books.

Stoneman, Z., & Brody, G.H. (1983). Immediate and long-term recognition and generalization of advertising products as a function of age and presentation mode. *Developmental Psychology.* 19: 56-61.

Straight talk on cell phones for children. *Consumer Reports,* February, 2006, 7.

Stutts, M.A., & Hunnicutt, G.G. (1987). Can young children understand disclaimers in television commercials? *Journal of Advertising.* 16: 41-46.

Subrahmanyam, K.; Greenfield, P. M.; Kraut, R.; & Gross, E. (2000). The Impact of computer use on children's development. *Media Usage Pattern,* 10: 123-144.

Summers, S. L. (2005). Get them thinking! Use media literacy to prepare students for state assessments. *Library Media Connection,* April-May, 20-23.

Sypeck, M.; Gray, J.; & Ahrens, A. (2003). No longer just a pretty face: fashion magazines' depictions of ideal female beauty from 1959 to 1999. *International Journal of Eating Disorders.* 36: 342-347.

Taylor, L. D. (2005). Effects of visual and verbal sexual television content and perceived realism on attitudes and beliefs. *The Journal of Sex Research,* 42: 130-137.

Tejeiro Salguero, R. A., & Bersabe Moran, R. M. (2002). Measuring problem video game playing in adolescents. *Society for the Study of Addiction to Alcohol and Other Drugs.* 97: 1601-1606.

The Parents' Guide to the Information Superhighway (1998). A Publication of The Children's Partnership with The National PTA and The National Urban League.

Thornburg, D., & Herbert, S. L. (2002). *Youth, Pornography, and the Internet.* Washington, DC: National Academy Press.

Tower, Roni; Singer, Dorothy; & Biggs, Ann (1979). Differential Effects of Television Programming on Preschoolers' Cognition, Imagination, and Social Play. *Orthopsychiatry.* 49: 2-5.

Trainor, Laurel J. (2004). Long-term memory for music: infants remember tempo and timbre. *Developmental Science.* 7: 289-296.

TV Parental Guidelines. Retrieved from *www.tvguidelines.org.*

Uhlmann, E., & Swanson, J. (2004). Exposure to violent video games increases automatic aggressiveness. *Journal of Adolescence.* 27: 41-52.

Valberg, P.; van Deventer, T.; & Repacholi, M. (2007). Workgroup Report: Base Stations and Wireless Networks-Radiofrequency (RF) Exposures and Health Consequences. *Environmental Health Perspectives.* 115: 416–424.

Valiero, M.; & Amodio, P. (1997). The Use of Television in 2-to 8-Year-Old Children and the Attitude of Parents About Such Use. Arch Pediatric *Adolescent Medicine.* 151: 22–26.

Valkenburg, P. M.; Schouten, A. P.; & Peter, J. (2005). Adolescents' identity experiments on the Internet. *New Media and Society,* 7: 383–402.

Valkenburg, Patti M., & Peter, Jochen (2007). Internet communication and its relation to well-being: Identifying some underlying mechanisms. *Media Psychology.* 9: 43–58.

Valkenburg, Patti M., & Peter, Jochen (2007). Preadolescents' and adolescents' online communication and their closeness to friends. *Developmental Psychology.* 43: 267–277.

Vandewater, E., & Bickham, D. (2007). Time well spent? Relating television use to children's free-time activity. *Pediatrics.* 117: 181–191.

Vandewater, E. A.; Shim, M.; & Caplovitz, A. G. (2004). Linking obesity and activity level with children's television and video game use. *Journal of Adolescence.* 27: 71–85.

Veal, M. L., & Ross, L. T. (2006). Gender, alcohol consumption, and parental monitoring. *The Journal of Psychology,* 140: 41–52.

Villani, S. (2001). Impact of media on children and adolescents: A 10-year review of the research. *Child Adolescence Psychiatry,* 40: 392–401.

Voracek, M., & Fisher, M. (2002). Shapely centerfolds? Temporal change in body measures: trend analysis. *Body Mass Journal,* 325: 21-28.

Walker, F. (2007). Primary workshop ideas for media literacy. *Screen Education,* 44: 84-88.

Wallenius, M.; Punamaki, R.; & Rimpela, A. (2006). Digital Game Playing and Direct and Indirect Aggression in Early Adolescence: The roles of age, social intelligence, and parent-child communication. *Springer Science and Business Media.* 36: 325-336.

Walling, J. I. (1976). The effect of parental interaction on learning from television. *Communication Education.* 25: 16-24.

Walma van Der Molen, J. (2003). Direct fright or worry? A survey of children's fear reactions to violence in fiction and news. International Communication Association, 2003 Annual Meeting, San Diego, CA, p1-28.

Wan, C., & Chiou, W. (2007). The motivations of adolescents who are addicted to online games: A cognitive perspective. *Adolescence.* 42: 180-197.

Wanamaker, C. E., & Reznikoff, M. (2001). Effects of aggressive and nonaggressive rock songs on projective and structured tests. *The Journal of Psychology,* 123: 561-570.

Warren, R. (2003). Parental mediation of preschool children's television viewing. *Journal of Broadcasting & Electronic Media.* 47: 394-417.

Weber, R.; Ritterfeld, U.; & Mathiak, K. (2006). Does playing violent video games induce aggression? Empirical evidence of a functional magnetic resonance imaging study. *Media Psychology.* 8: 39-60.

Weiss, D. L. (2007). Children and pornography. *www.family.org/socialissues/A0000001155.cfm.*

Wharton, Mandell (1985). Violence on television and imitative behavior: Impact on parenting practices. *Pediatrics.* 75: 1120–1123.

What is media literacy? (2007). Alliance for a media literate America. Safety by age. *www.kids.getnetwise.org/safteyguide.*

Wilson, B.; Smith, S.; Potter, J.; Kunkel, D.; Linz, D.; & Colvin, C. (2002). Violence in Children's Television Programming: Assessing the Risks. *Journal of Communication,* 52: 6–35.

Withrow, F. B. (2004). *Literacy in the Digital Age: Reading, Writing, Viewing, and Computing.* Lanham, MD: Scarecrow Education.

Wolak, J.; Mitchell, K. J.; and Finkelhor, D. (2002). Close online relationships in a national sample of adolescents. *Adolescence,* 37: 441–455.

Wood, R.; Griffiths, M.; & Parke, A. (2006). Experiences of Time Loss among Videogame Players: An Empirical Study. *CyberPsychology & Behavior.* 10: 38–44.

Woodard, E., & Mares, K. (2005). Positive effects of television on children's social interactions: A meta-analysis. *Media Psychology,* 7: 301–322.

Yan, Z. (2005). Age differences in children's understanding of the complexity of the Internet. *Applied Developmental Psychology,* 26: 385–396.

Zimmerman, F. J., & Christakis, D. A. (2007). Television and DVD/Video viewing in children younger than two years. *Archives of Pediatrics and Adolescent Medicine,* 161: 473–479.

Zogby, J.; Bruce, J.; & Wittman, R. (2006). Survey of teens and adults aboutt the use of personal electronic devices and headphones. Submitted to the American Speech-Language-Hearing Association.

Zukerman, D., & Zukerman, B. (1985). Television's Impact on Children. *Pediatrics.* 75: 2.

Index